REVISED AND ENLARGED EDITION

Isles of the
CARIBBEES

by Carleton Mitchell

FOREWORD BY MELVILLE BELL GROSVENOR
Editor-in-Chief, National Geographic Society

PREPARED BY THE SPECIAL PUBLICATIONS DIVISION
Robert L. Breeden, Chief

NATIONAL GEOGRAPHIC SOCIETY
WASHINGTON, D.C.

ISLES OF THE CARIBBEES
by Carleton Mitchell

Published by
The National Geographic Society
Melvin M. Payne,
President
Melville Bell Grosvenor,
Editor-in-Chief
Gilbert M. Grosvenor,
Editor

James Cerruti,
Consulting Editor

Prepared by
The Special Publications Division
Robert L. Breeden, *Editor*
Donald J. Crump, *Associate Editor*
Philip B. Silcott, *Manuscript Editor*
Cynthia Russ Ramsay, Johanna G. Farren,
  Research
Mary Ann Harrell, *Style*
Michael E. Long, William L. Allen,
  Picture Editors
Joseph A. Taney, *Art Director*
Josephine B. Bolt, *Assistant Art Director*
Ursula Perrin, *Design Assistant*
Betty Cloninger, John D. Garst, Jr.,
  Monica T. Woodbridge, *Map Research
  and Production*
Ronald M. Fisher, Robert W. Messer,
  Production
Gail Farmer, Ann H. Crouch,
  Production Assistants
James R. Whitney, John R. Metcalfe,
  Engraving and Printing
Editorial Staff: Linda Bridge, Mary Ann
  Harrell, Geraldine Linder, Gerald S.
  Snyder, Peggy D. Winston
Staff Assistants: Tucker L. Etherington,
  Suzanne J. Jacobson, Raja D. Murshed,
  Donna Rey Naame, Joan Perry,
  Suzanne B. Thompson
Anne K. McCain, Toni Jean Warner, *Index*

Steel band keeps the tempo for a parade on St. Thomas in the U. S. Virgin Islands. Overleaf: A rainbow arcs
above a sea-going yawl off verdant St.
Lucia. Page 1: Author Carleton Mitchell explores an underwater trail on
Buck Island Reef near St. Croix. Book-
binding: *Sans Terre,* a "home afloat."

NATIONAL GEOGRAPHIC PHOTOGRAPHERS JAMES L. STANFIELD
(RIGHT AND PAGE 1) AND WINFIELD PARKS (OVERLEAF)

Foreword

THIS BOOK was born on blue water. Fresh trades were pushing us across Anegada Passage in a rhythmic rush. I was standing watch with skipper Carleton Mitchell on his 38-foot yawl *Finisterre* during his cruise from Grenada to St. Thomas.

Mitch felt like talking. And because he is a truly great storyteller—who had written evocatively of the Caribbean in the past—I shared the mood. Our conversation ranged as wide as the sea: modern ports and vanished pirates, rich plantations, shipwrecks, fine meals and fishing trips, sea battles, sudden storms.

"Wonderful yarns!" I said at last. "Mitch, you have to write another book!"

Happily, he did. With *Isles of the Caribbees* he reached a wide and diverse public; the book guided not only the jet-age tourists but also the yachtsmen who cruised there in their own and chartered boats. More than that, it steered those questing spirits who used it as their passage to one of the world's most romantic regions.

Now he has returned once more, to record the changes brought about by the rapid growth and development of the islands. In writing this new edition of *Isles of the Caribbees*, he revisited ports throughout the Caribbean. As I leaf through its pages I can all but hear Mitch's voice, and taste the salt of ocean spray from that earlier voyage.

There was Brimstone Hill towering upon St. Kitts. We climbed it at dawn, that "Gibraltar of the West Indies." From the 750-foot summit, we admired a dazzling view of bright channels and the isles of Statia and Saba. And then our friend Lt. Col. Henry Howard, Administrator of St. Kitts, told us the story of the islands' turbulent past.

Angered by the Dutch salute to the new U. S. flag at Statia in the year 1776, British Admiral Rodney sacked its rich port—seizing many ships and stores of British and St. Kitts' merchants. Retaliating, Colonel Howard told us, the Kittitians refused to help British troops carry cannon up to Brimstone Hill Fort in the face of an impending French attack. We could almost see the 1,200 defending Redcoats—and imagine their despair when their own guns below were turned against them by the 6,000 besieging French. The British fought bravely before finally surrendering.

With Mitch, I tried skin diving for the first time. And I must admit that my undersea view of the shipwreck *Rocas* was one of the eeriest experiences of my life. This freighter, sunk on Horse Shoe Reef around 1929, still carries a grisly cargo: the bones and grinning skulls of horses.

On Peter Island, we explored that pirate haunt Deadman Bay and the desolate cay named Dead Chest. One view of the bleak setting, and my favorite sea chant took on new meaning: "Fifteen men on the dead man's chest. . . ." By tradition, Blackbeard left mutineers stranded here.

Such are the rich details that bring glamour to forgotten rocks and make history breathe anew. Here is the whole West Indies—as varied as Europe, with its isles so strongly French, Dutch, English.

Only Carleton Mitchell could have done this volume. He writes as he sails—intensely, with great ardor and flair. We would cruise all night, Mitch navigating, standing his watch, and skippering to boot. Then at dawn he would go ashore to spend the day interviewing people, collecting notes.

This new *Isles of the Caribbees* retains the magic of the first edition while updating that version and enlarging it for today's travelers. It is my pleasure to welcome each reader aboard. *Bon voyage.*

Melville Bell Grosvenor

Tinged with gold by early-morning sun, fishing nets swing from drying poles on Martinique. Islanders

Contents

...using seines like these reap the sea's harvest off uncounted beaches throughout the isles of the Caribbees.

I *Grenada:*
Gateway to the Windwards

Cloud-shadowed hills cradle anchorages at St. George's, capital of Grenada. From this "Isle of Spice,"

*F*ROM AFAR Grenada seemed unchanged. It appeared in late afternoon as a pale silhouette lifting above the horizon, scarcely more tangible than the piled trade-wind clouds. As the blue haze of distance melted, the jagged outline transmuted into mountains, and valleys appeared as shadowed slashes. Still closer, the blue became green, the rich sensuous green of the tropics, accented by red roofs peeping through the trees. For me, the unfolding beauty and excitement of an island landfall will never lose its magic.

Finally over the bow of my ocean cruiser *Sans Terre* lay the town of St. George's. Passing under old Fort George, I was suddenly in the harbor. Once again I had the feeling of entering a theater after the curtain had gone up. Sloops and schooners were moored along a horseshoe quay lined by shops and warehouses. Behind, like a painted backdrop, pastel houses fanned out over encircling hills.

It was the same as when I had sailed in almost a quarter of a century before aboard *Carib*, the 47-foot ketch that was my first offshore cruiser. Yet it was not the same. There was the familiar aroma of nutmeg and mace—Grenada remains the "Isle of Spice." Rowboats used as water taxis continued lazily to cross the harbor, offering an alternative to the long walk around the quays. But now there seemed a quickening of the pulse, a new sense of movement.

Perhaps it was due to the clamorous automobile traffic ashore, or the proliferation of dwellings on the slopes above, or the sight of a hundred yachts in the inner lagoon, but even from the deck of *Sans Terre* I sensed that a new era had dawned for the Isles of the Caribbees.

I was not wrong. During the next three

author Carleton Mitchell set out on his most recent cruise of the Windward and Leeward Islands.

months I was to find that the islands are moving rapidly ahead, although the timetable is not everywhere identical. Some are just beginning to stir. Fishing villages still drowse under a frieze of palms, where naked children scamper in and out of the shallows, and there are beaches unprinted by footsteps. On remote mountainsides farmers live in huts and cultivate tiny plots carved from the forest, as did their forefathers. Yet to the interweaving of races, languages, and customs stemming from the romantic past has been added a new awareness of identity and destiny.

I was embarking on my third voyage among the islands. My first came immediately after World War II, when the West Indies still slumbered in the colonial era. Then, 18 years later, in 1965, I returned to sail along the chain in *Finisterre*, a 38-foot centerboard yawl with an ocean-racing record that included an unprecedented

triple victory in the Newport-to-Bermuda classic. And now I was back, to see what had happened in the meantime to my favorite cruising area.

"Changes since your last visit?" repeated the dynamic Premier of Grenada, the Honourable Eric M. Gairy, when I raised the question. "Grenada is no longer a colony of Britain. We fly our own flag, and are responsible to no one else for the conduct of our internal affairs. Outside investors are aiding our development, diversifying the economy, and opening new fields of employment. Improved communications bring us closer to the world, and the world to us. You can say there have been more changes here in the last four years than in the last century."

In 1967 Grenada became one of the six Associated States of the West Indies, and a member of the British Commonwealth. Under the new constitution Britain retains

NATIONAL GEOGRAPHIC PHOTOGRAPHER JAMES L. STANFIELD

PAINTING BY HEINRICH BERANN

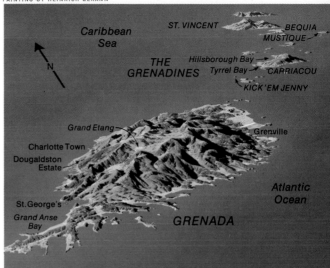

Alone on the flying bridge, the author puts his new 42-foot powerboat *Sans Terre,* built in Hong Kong, through her paces in Caribbean waters. Grenada (map, above) is the southernmost island of the 250-mile-long Windward chain.

responsibility only for defense and external affairs, but continues to provide economic aid. The next step may well be full independence, a status already gained by neighboring Barbados and the island state of Trinidad and Tobago. While I had been aware of the emerging nations of Africa and Asia, I was slow to realize that a similar process was taking place on the United States' Caribbean doorstep.

As though to underline the new dynamism, the opening of CARIFTA Expo '69, one of the first international fairs held in the West Indies, coincided with my arrival on Grenada. "Yes, we still revel in our equable temperatures. Our steep green mountains. Our beaches. . . . Fishing, yachting, snorkeling and water-skiing will be with us as always," I read in an Expo brochure as a taxi sped along a new double highway. "But Grenada has other things on her mind. . . . so, we're rolling up our sleeves. For self-development."

Billed as the "Showcase of Caribbean Progress," Expo '69 included exhibits of the 11 nations forming CARIFTA, the Caribbean Free Trade Association. Members among the Windward and Leeward group are Grenada, St. Vincent, St. Lucia, Dominica, Antigua, Montserrat, and the state of St. Kitts-Nevis-Anguilla. Others include Barbados and Jamaica and the state of Trinidad and Tobago. There is even a segment of South America, Guyana.

While neither a customs union nor a common market, CARIFTA marks an important step toward economic integration. Within months after the agreement became effective in mid-1968, a major proportion of island commerce was relieved of import duties and quotas. Further reductions are scheduled, with the goal of completely free trade in ten years. Many islanders hope such trade will eventually lead to a form of political federation.

Although the fair had not been formally opened, a policeman at the gate waved my taxi inside. Never had I seen West Indians working so fast. Painters wielded brushes on boards even as carpenters nailed them into place; electricians strung wires overhead; gardeners planted shrubbery. Across

11

NATIONAL GEOGRAPHIC PHOTOGRAPHERS WINFIELD PARKS (ABOVE) AND DEAN CONGER

Sunlight and mace flow through skilled fingers of women grading the aromatic spice in a plant at Charlotte Town, on Grenada's leeward coast. Mace grows as a ruby cloak on ripe nutmeg (left); if unbroken when removed, the fibrous cover brings a higher price. Workers (right) crack nutmeg shells and sack kernels for export. Grenada's volcanic soil also produces cloves, cinnamon, cacao, and fragrant tonka beans.

'69. Hundreds of Grenadians had worked day and night to transform a 225-acre peninsula into a fairground. Roads had been built, pavilions erected, facilities provided.

Part of the ambitious undertaking could not be finished in time, but I was greatly impressed by what had been accomplished. I was equally impressed by displays of goods already manufactured by some CARIFTA members, reflecting the effort to break away from a centuries-old dependence on agriculture. In the pavilions I saw pottery, garden tools, underclothing, refined petroleum products, furniture, soap, tinned biscuits, and perfume.

On my return to St. George's I strolled

the road roustabouts struggled to erect a ferris wheel in Fun City, taking form behind a banner proclaiming: "Coney Island of Puerto Rico."

Entering a building marked "Information," I was met by Frances Slinger, an acquaintance from a former visit. "Grab a brush or a broom!" she greeted me. Later, she told me that all I was seeing had been done in five months, after Premier Gairy had conceived the idea of CARIFTA Expo

familiar streets. Behind a watermelon rind of beach washed by the open Caribbean, the houses rise abruptly to flow over a rollercoaster hill and drop to Carenage Town, which rims the inner harbor. In 1895 tunnel builders pierced the hill, but citizens and visitors alike prefer the streets, with a glint of water at each end.

Since my first visit, St. George's has lived in my mind as the perfect West Indian capital, from the dim shops behind the waterfront to the gingerbread majesty of Government House on the hilltop above. Now I found I could buy frozen food at reasonable copies of American supermarkets. But the open-air market remains, as always, the pulsing heart of a simple community.

Pushing my way through, I became part of the remembered swirl of color and smell and sound. Around me upended boxes and trestle tables displayed not only exotic tropic produce but also the familiar staples of the temperate zones. Among mounds of breadfruit, mangoes, pigeon peas, and plantains, I found carrots, potatoes, onions, tomatoes, and corn. Children scampered underfoot, dogs barked, and tethered chickens pecked at fallen scraps.

As though I were seeing a familiar film rerun, a dark hand extended three golden oranges. "Here de best, mistah," called a voice in the softly slurred accents of the islands. "De mon want bananas," interposed another vendor. "Look yere, sah!"

"Look, sah!" became a chorus, and soon I had filled a coconut-fiber basket bought at another booth. I paid in Eastern Caribbean Currency (E.C.C. dollars), which has replaced the old British West Indies ("Bee-Wee") currency of colonial days. The new dollars, however, remained tied to the pound sterling and dropped to an exchange rate of two for each U. S. dollar when Britain devalued the pound.

On my way out, I stopped at a refreshment stand for my favorite hot-country beverage—the liquid in a green coconut. After I had pointed to my choice atop a mound, the vendor took the nut in his left hand. There was a flash as he swung a razor-sharp cutlass in his other hand, and I was proffered a goblet of the gods.

Drinking from the coconut, with sunshine like a friendly warm hand on my shoulder, I felt more than ever a part of the world around me. Much of my life I

Oyster-white sand of Grand Anse Beach slips through shadowy coconut palms to the sea, welcoming cooling trade winds and inviting a stroll by children with pet goats. Below, a smiling girl reflects the warmth of her island in the sun.

have spent among the islands lying in a lazy arc between Trinidad and Florida. I knew that many of the women behind the displays of fruit and vegetables had left their tiny gardens before dawn, plodding down steep dark paths with baskets on their heads. Some waited beside the road for an island bus—a flatbed truck with a home-made body and wooden planks for seats, bearing a name like Island Fancy, Take-it-Easy, Angel Guardian, or Creole Pride.

For these folk, the market was more than a way to earn a few dollars: It was a place to gossip, to pass the news of births and deaths, to greet old friends and make new ones. Even bargaining was a ritual to be savored by both buyer and seller. Watching and listening, I was content in the certainty that despite changes to come the things I liked best about the West Indies would endure: the basic simplicity of the people, the almost perfect weather, the beauty of the islands themselves.

No work of fiction is more fantastic than the history of the streaming of life from the Old World to the New. The astronauts of Apollo 11 knew far more of what they would find when they stepped onto the moon than did the early explorers setting forth in cranky small ships, at the mercy of unknown winds and currents.

Of the bold adventurers who wove a tapestry of romance with their keels, none seems as great to me as Christopher Columbus. He wrought superhuman feats of seamanship and discovery despite human frailties and the superstitions of his era. Courageous captains and crews followed in his wake, probing and prodding. Those who lived to return scratched bits of shore-line on pieces of parchment until maps took form. Behind them came the others—colonists, traders, soldiers, farmers, priests, and buccaneers, superimposing a facsimile of their own civilization on the peoples and lands they found.

There are names which roll down through the centuries like mighty ocean swells from the past. Pierre Belain, Sieur d'Esnambuc, planted the fleur-de-lis under

the tropic sun. Peter Stuyvesant lost a leg in a battle off Sint Maarten before going on to that more northerly Dutch settlement, Nieuw Amsterdam.

The Elizabethan freebooter Sir Francis Drake gave his name to the channel in the Virgin Islands through which he passed to attack San Juan in 1595; and that other famed freebooter, Sir John Hawkins, died on the same expedition and was buried at sea. Later came other naval heroes, names to conjure visions for every boy: Hood and Rodney and Nelson.

Then there were the inhabitants the early explorers and settlers found and fought, the fiercely savage Caribs, sometimes written as Charaibes or Caribbees in old accounts, whom Columbus called "Indians." Not long before the arrival of the first Europeans the Caribs came out of the Amazon jungles of Brazil to flow northward by canoe, overcoming an earlier people, the less warlike Arawaks, devouring the males captured in battle and taking their women. *Caniba*, the Arawakan name for the

Caribs, gives us the dread word "cannibal."

By the time Columbus arrived on his second voyage in 1493, the Caribs had reached the Virgin Islands, where they were stalled by the sheer number of Arawaks on the land mass of Puerto Rico. Although Columbus was greeted by the Caribs' poisoned arrows on his second arrival in the New World, rather than by the friendliness the Arawaks accorded him when he first set foot in the Bahamas, it was the Caribs who gave their name to the sea.

It was partly to follow again the island-hopping migration of the Caribs that I had started my cruise at Grenada. While the geographic pattern ahead was simple, the terminology was not. Through the centuries an overlapping of names has occurred, confusing to old hand and newcomer alike.

On his first voyage Columbus thought he had arrived in the Indies, an archipelago off the coast of Asia. He therefore referred to the islands he saw as *Las Yndias Ocidentales*—the West Indies.

In a tug-of-war with the rolling surf, fishermen on Grenada's Grand Mal Beach haul in a seine heavy with sharp-nosed bait-fish called ballyhoo (below). Thrusting above newly planked fishing schooners, coconut palms bend to trade winds that blow almost ceaselessly among the emerald-green islands of the West Indies. Warm waters of the archipelago also yield dolphin and bonito.

Renaissance cartographers, remembering the legendary lost land of Antillia, showed the islands on some maps as the Antilles. Accordingly, Puerto Rico and the larger islands to the west became the Greater Antilles, and the eastern islands became the Lesser Antilles.

Early Spanish navigators made their division in terms of the prevailing easterly breezes, which regulated their sailing. Those islands eastward from Puerto Rico, in the teeth of the trade winds, were *Islas de Barlovento*, the Windward Islands. Those downwind, including the islands off the coast of South America, were *Islas de Sotavento*, the Leewards.

The English, although a maritime nation, upset this logical division when they acquired most of the islands between Grenada and Puerto Rico. For administrative purposes, they split them into two groups, the Windwards and the Leewards, whose dividing line often shifted. But in terms of the trade winds, the British Leewards lie to windward of the British Windwards!

As a further complication, the Dutch call their three northern islands—Saba, Sint Eustatius, and Sint Maarten—the Netherlands Windward Islands because they are northeast of Curaçao; yet they lie among the British Leewards!

Today, however, naming groups of islands in terms of the prevailing breeze or colonial political pattern has less meaning. Planes and engine-driven ships pay slight attention to the direction of the wind, and former colonies are becoming independent states. Undoubtedly a future island federation will put a new name on the map, but I will always think of the stepping-stones from Grenada through the Virgin Islands simply as the Isles of the Caribbees.

Grenada epitomizes the southern islands of the chain, a volcanic mass rising steeply to a crater on a central spine of mountains. Out of St. George's a road dating from the French occupation of the 17th and 18th centuries spirals upward. As my rented Volkswagen growled on the hairpin curves, lush vegetation pressed in from both sides. Waxy dark-green leaves of breadfruit alternated with the delicate tracery of coconut-palm fronds. Poinsettia and bougainvillea added splashes of color. Then the sun vanished as I came to uplands almost perpetually damp from enveloping clouds.

Near a sign showing an elevation of 1,910 feet, a narrow road branched off. Wrapped in chill mist as penetrating as New England fog, I had an end-of-the-world feeling. The ghosts of Carib warriors seemed to be flitting among the trees as I neared the Grand Etang, the crater lake. Suddenly, where I had thought to be alone, I found myself in the middle of an outing—my Carib warriors were small boys, equally surprised to find an invading stranger.

"We on picnic," explained a broadly smiling matron who was tending a huge iron pot of chicken and rice, or *pelau*, while other pots bubbled on charcoal braziers.

Raven-haired carnival queen swims in sparkling water of a mountain pool below Annandale Falls near St. George's. Ferns peek from the spray and philodendrons climb the rocks.

I repeated what she had said, not once but several times, unable to understand a word. As sometimes happens, local pronunciation can sound like a wholly unfamiliar language.

The woman finally called, "Francis!" From a bus named Trinity of Sauteurs a man approached. In his hand was a paperback book, *The Story of Jesus.* He explained that I had stumbled upon the annual picnic of the Moyah Baptist Church.

"We on picnic," the woman said again, with an I-tried-to-tell-you-so air. Suddenly I understood. The woman began to laugh. Everyone standing nearby whooped. I laughed hardest of all. The ability to laugh —and especially at yourself—is the surest way to make friends in the West Indies.

Accompanied by Francis and a trailing convoy of giggling children I walked down to the shore. The brownish water of the Grand Etang reflected clouds racing over the cup of surrounding hills. From reeds bordering the lake frogs piped tiny musical notes resembling distant chimes. It was a peaceful moment, far removed from the mighty volcanic convulsions that long ago had created the islands.

More recent volcanic activity left Grenada with a legacy of rich soil. Again I visited Dougaldston Estate, which produces bananas, coconuts, cacao, nutmeg, mace, cloves, cinnamon, pimento, and saffron for export, plus some coffee for local consumption. I was greeted by William Allan Branch, son of the planter who had shown me around before. "My father was manager from 1908 until his death last year, when I took over," he explained.

My first question stemmed from the passage of Hurricane Janet in September 1955. Although Grenada is south of the usual track of the storm centers, Janet struck the island with devastating force, flattening houses and stripping whole hillsides. "Grenada was like a plucked chicken," a survivor told me. "Everywhere you looked at bare earth." For an island dependent almost wholly on the export of agricultural products, it was a disaster. Although two lesser storms have passed nearby in the

Grenadian on a slalom ski skims a wake off St. George's. Island waters lure deep-sea fishers, skin divers, and yachtsmen. Children born to the sea swim as easily as they sprint the sands.

last few years, Janet is still referred to locally as *the* hurricane.

"Our output of nutmeg has never recovered," Mr. Branch told me. "We lost almost 70 percent of our trees. Only the females produce, and it takes five or six years for a tree to 'declare,' or blossom. Then most of the male trees are removed, and the bearing female trees spaced. It is a slow process, taking 15 years in all, and we simply haven't been able to get enough labor. As the tourist trade increases, workers leave the soil."

Cacao production was back to pre-Janet levels. We passed aromatic vats where the beans "sweat" away a fibrous outer covering under a blanket of banana leaves. Farther along, we came upon large shallow trays where the cacao is sun-dried. A middle-aged woman was turning the beans with a wooden rake. Leaving Mr. Branch, I walked closer to watch.

"You have to stir when de cocoa damp," Alice James volunteered with a smile, "den when it dry we tramples with de feet to give de beans a glass—a polish."

Remembering a ritual no longer practiced, I asked, "How do you dance cocoa?" Her smile became broader, and she broke into a shuffle. Her hips moved in a sinuous version of the mambo, and her feet rolled the beans against the smooth pine planks. "In de old days de men would come with a drum, and we danced until de beans shine to make dem look pretty, den went away happy with de work."

Inside a nearby building, I found women sitting in a circle on the floor. So rapidly it was hard for the eye to follow, each would take a nutmeg from a pile in the center and strip away the Chinese-red outer covering of the jet-black shell. The fiber was packed in small baskets, and the stripped nuts were tossed onto another pile.

Smiling grandstand belles chat excitedly during a race at Seamoon Track near Grenville, on Grenada's eastern shore. Railbirds at left crowd the infield fence to watch their favorites pound past the starter. Island-bred horses race at Seamoon and at Barbados and Trinidad tracks.

Catching the eye of a worker, I asked her to explain. "We calls dis de 'skirt' or 'dress' of de nutmeg. You calls it 'mace,' another spice."

Rising, she volunteered to be my guide. "My name is Boopsingh, so ever'body calls me 'Baby,'" she said. A tiny woman blinking like a bird behind large glasses, Baby told me she was of Indian descent. Her grandfather had been an indentured worker, brought from India after Britain abolished slavery in the colonies in 1834. The influx of Indians in the 19th century contributed to the mixture of races and cultures that adds flavor to the islands.

In theory the Caribbean became a Spanish lake soon after its discovery. In 1494 the Treaty of Tordesillas divided the non-Christian overseas world between Spain and Portugal. Spain received all territories west of a line drawn at approximately 50 degrees longitude, which gave it

not only the islands but also North America and most of South America. The treaty gave Portugal claim to Brazil.

The other maritime nations of Europe scoffed at the division. Soon the English, French, Dutch, and Danes were sailing almost where they pleased. In 1624 the first English colony settled on St. Kitts. Rival nations quickly staked out colonies, and for two centuries played a game of musical islands to the tune of cannon fire against a background of diplomacy. Africans were brought in to till the plantations, and, after the abolition of slavery, many indentured Indian workers arrived.

In Grenada variety extends to terrain and climate. One day I swam in a mountain pool below Annandale Falls. The approach road runs northeast from St. George's through walls of green. Chill water cascaded onto my head as I gasped for breath. The next day, with the keeper

21

Forbidding needles of the prickly-pear cactus *(Opuntia)* guard fragile yellow blossoms set aglow by the island sun. Sweet-scented frangipani (above) blooms in clusters, its overlapping petals curling at the edges. In Latin America, bougainvillea (left) sometimes takes the name *trinitaria* because three showy bracts cup each tiny flower.

of the Point Salines lighthouse, James Eddy, I looked down on a cactus-studded desert at the southwestern tip of the island. "Sometimes here we goes for weeks without rain, even when we can't see St. George's or the mountains for the clouds."

Other less sere peninsulas on the southern end have mushroomed with homes, many built by American and Canadian visitors who decided to settle. Those who bought early were lucky. Grenada, like almost every other island I would visit, was experiencing a boom in land values, especially for beach property. "When available, it brings at least one dollar U. S. per square foot, sold by the acre. That amounts to $43,560, a pretty penny for unimproved land," commented O'Brien Donovan, a real-estate broker. "In smaller lots, the price is frequently higher. But almost nothing is for sale."

He laughed at my incredulous expression, and continued, "In 1916 I was an officer in the Agriculture Bureau. We tried to sell land on Grand Anse Beach—where the hotels are going up—at $2.50 U. S. an acre. Nobody would buy until the government planted coconut trees: Only crop-producing land had any value."

Another boom I had noticed on my previous visit showed indications of a possible slowdown. On Grenada, as on all the other islands, children are everywhere—torrents of children. The population explosion has visibly arrived. Schools, medical facilities, housing, and employment opportunities, though expanding, will be hard-pressed to keep pace with a population which has been increasing at a rate above 2 percent— when 3 percent means a doubling in just 23 years.

At CARIFTA Expo '69 the Grenada pavilion featured displays of the Planned Parenthood Association. Posters warned of future hardships and shortages in education, employment, and housing if the island population were not kept in check.

"We've been active for five years, but only recently have we seen real results," said Mrs. Joyce Lyder, a volunteer worker. "Originally we ran into opposition, but people are coming around to the idea. The birth rate is down from 44 per 1,000 to 29."

Arriving for a visit at Government House, I passed the sentry box at the gate and saw the flag of Grenada—with blue, gold, and green horizontal bars and a nutmeg in the center—waving proudly in the breeze, replacing the British ensign. Yet I found that the island has not severed its sentimental ties with the mother country. After I entered the stately mansion, built in 1852, when young Queen Victoria ruled an empire on which the sun never set, ermine-robed figures looked down on me from portraits on the walls.

I was received by Dame Hilda Bynoe, the only woman governor in the Caribbean. From Dame Hilda I learned that the political structure of Grenada and the other Associated States is like a miniature of England's. The leader of the party gaining the most seats in the ten-member House of Representatives in an election becomes Premier and chooses a Cabinet. There is also a nine-member Senate appointed by the governor. It is the elected government which makes the decisions.

"My position is similar to that of Queen Elizabeth," explained Dame Hilda. "Government House and the governor are no longer symbols of power, but of the hopes and aspirations of the people. Previous to my appointment by the Queen, I was a doctor, practicing principally in Trinidad and

Pulp of a cacao pod hides beans that will become chocolate after workers ferment them in "sweating sheds," then spread them in the sun to dry. Five million chocolate trees grow on Grenada.

British Guiana after training in London. I was never involved in politics – which might have been a qualification that weighed with both the local party and the Crown."

As I took my leave, I paused on the veranda to look down on the harbor of St. George's, where perhaps the greatest change of all had taken place since my last visit. In 1960 a channel was dredged through a reef barring entrance to a natural lagoon adjoining the deep commercial port. A virtually stormproof shelter for small craft was created, inviting the building of a marina and a repair facility.

In 1965 *Finisterre* had shared the docks with only a few other floating nomads. Now greatly extended quays were chock-a-block, and the overflow anchored off as a densely packed fleet. While many were private vessels, the majority represented a recent phenomenon – the charter yacht.

"You can take your choice from a 30-foot 'bareboat' – the nautical equivalent of a drive-yourself automobile – to a 110-foot schooner with a crew of seven," I was told by Robert C. Petersen, general manager of Grenada Yacht Services, Ltd. "Approximately 60 charter vessels are permanently based in Grenada. The average rate is $1,400 U. S. per week, and we estimate each party spends another $200 on taxis, shopping, and the rest. If every yacht was chartered only 12 weeks a year, it would mean $1,152,000 U. S. entering the economy. And that is not counting money spent by private yachts or vessels chartered in

Bluff headlands—broken rim of a volcanic crater—guard the harbor of St. George's. Beyond the 800-foot pier where ocean-going freighters berth, yachts throng a modern marina. Water taxis ferry passengers to and fro, oarsman Biran Joseph Cox (above, in his rowboat *Mae West*) has plied this route for 40 years.

other islands which make St. George's a port of call. There are almost a hundred yachts in the lagoon today."

Among them lay my new boat. Much thought and soul-searching had gone into the transition from *Finisterre* to *Sans Terre*, the step from a wind-driven ocean cruiser-racer to a diesel-powered ocean cruiser-home afloat. From without, *Sans Terre* looked like a fishing trawler, bluff of bow and rugged, innocent of gleaming varnish and polished brass. Below, she was a lady. A Grand Banks 42 built in Hong Kong by American Marine, Ltd., she had been modified and fitted with extras in accordance with my specifications. Chinese craftsmen, combining Oriental hardwoods and the latest equipment, had fashioned a

vessel for both long range and comfort.

Although only 42 feet over-all, she has three sleeping areas, plus two heads with showers—a determining factor in my shift from sail to power had been a desire to provide privacy for crew members. Aft of the forward stateroom lies the main cabin, the community center. It provides not only a sheltered lower steering station, but also a galley comparable to the kitchen of a small house. Windows open on a vista to the horizon. Cabin bulkheads and furniture are of softly finished teak.

By day, the after stateroom becomes a study with a file cabinet, a typing desk, and shelves for reference books. But as the name *Sans Terre* means "free from the land," ample fuel tanks are tucked in, along

25

with an evaporator to distill drinking water from the sea. A deep freeze and a refrigerator assure supplies for weeks at a time.

Waiting on deck and ready to get under way was my crew, Alvin Daniels and his wife Eula. We had already put astern more than 7,000 miles since leaving their home port of Newport Beach, California.

As before, on leaving St. George's, I was reminded of the Mediterranean. Looking back, I saw a pocket of blue water sheltered behind a jutting peninsula topped by a stone fortress, and, beyond, a rim of pastel houses set into a green backdrop of hillside. St. George's is a Caribbean version of my beloved Portofino, on Italy's Riviera.

Strangely, fate had made the bond between the towns deeper than mere physical resemblance. I learned the story from Charles ("Laddie") McIntyre, then Commodore of the Grenada Yacht Club. In 1961 an Italian cruise ship, the *Bianca C.*, burst into flame while anchored off Grenada. Wailing sirens had turned a Sunday-morning race around the buoys into a race to the stricken vessel.

"By the time our little sailboats got there, along with every other craft in the harbor, the ship was being abandoned," Laddie had related. "Fire had followed an explosion in the engine room. It spread so fast that many escaped with nothing but the clothes they were wearing. Our people cared for over 600 survivors until another ship could be sent to pick them up."

In appreciation the Italian shipowners gave the people of St. George's a statue. Swinging close to its rock pedestal on the shore, I once again saw the replica of the famous Christ of the Deep, which stands submerged off the monastery of San Fruttuoso—almost in Portofino's front yard.

Outside the harbor *Sans Terre* turned northward on water glassy calm. We seemed to be hanging in space, the sea blue below and the sky equally blue above, while the shoreline slid astern as though painted on a revolving screen. Smooth water on the Caribbean side of the islands is a phenomenon of Windward Island cruising.

Since winds are almost invariably from the east—the same reliable trades which wafted commerce and settlers from Europe to the Americas during the age of sail—the western coasts lie in the wind shadow of the mountains. Here the first colonists were able to land, and here blossomed the most important towns.

While still in the lee calm, we passed a yawl lying almost motionless under limp sails. Relaxed on the flying bridge, we waved, knowing her turn would come soon, for another side of Windward Island cruising lay just ahead, where the land ended.

Caribs Leap: In 1650, Carib warriors attacked by the French hurled their women and children into the sea at Grenada's northern tip, and then jumped after them rather than surrender. Dominican Father Paul Demajo strolls near the cliff, site of St. Patrick's Roman Catholic Church.

Christ of the Deep: A bronze replica of the underwater statue off San Fruttuoso, Italy, stands in St. George's harbor. The gift of Italian shipowners, it expresses gratitude for the care Grenadians gave survivors of a vessel that had sunk nearby in 1961.

II *The Grenadines:*
Of Sailors and the Sea

Kick 'em Jenny: Pounded by boat-swallowing currents, the rock north of Grenada lives up to a bellicose

O N THE DOORSTEP of the Grenadines lies a conical islet which has been a stumbling block for sailing ships through the centuries. Although it is shown on some charts as Diamond Islet, no local sailor calls it anything but Kick 'em Jenny.

There are two theories behind the origin of the nickname. Both pay tribute to its cantankerous qualities. More-scholarly islanders believe the name stems from a corruption of the French, *cay qui gêne,* "the troublesome cay," because currents swirling around the base gave the old windjammers such a hard time. Others say it's Kick 'em Jenny because the surrounding seas pack such a fierce wallop.

Once out of the lee calm of Grenada, we encountered another characteristic of Windward Islands cruising—rough water between islands. When the trade winds blow fresh, pushing along swells which have rolled unbroken from the coast of Africa, wind-driven hillocks come on soundings and are stirred by the giant eggbeater of tidal currents. A wicked sea is the inevitable result. As we crossed the unprotected channel and *Sans Terre* began to buck, I felt that Kick 'em Jenny had more in

nickname. Sailors say the waters kick like a donkey around the cliff, called Diamond Islet on some charts.

NATIONAL GEOGRAPHIC PHOTOGRAPHER DEAN CONGER

common with a bronco than with a donkey.

Around the base of the desolate volcanic outcropping seas crashed into wind-borne spume; above, seabirds rose screaming from crevices. It was a sight unchanged from the day the first Carib canoe had passed boldly toward the north.

Aloof on a bank of soundings extending some 50 miles between Grenada and St. Vincent, the Grenadines, an archipelago of more than 100 scattered islands and rocks, had seemed to me destined to drowse forever. Previously the least-visited of the Windwards, the islands four years earlier had been accessible only by roving yacht or waddling mail boat whose passengers shared the deck with produce and livestock. So simple had been the view of the world held by many residents of one isolated island, Carriacou, that they often referred to Grenada as "the mainland."

Now, as Kick 'em Jenny dropped astern and Carriacou lifted ahead, I saw a sight impossible four years earlier: A twin-engine plane descended from the sky and disappeared behind a hill in what was obviously a routine landing.

"An airport on Carriacou!" I exclaimed to my old friend J. Linton Rigg, as I came ashore at Hillsborough Bay.

Linton chuckled. A former yacht designer and broker, ex-member of the War Shipping Administration, and one of the all-time greats of ocean racing, Linton had retired on Carriacou after exploring the Caribbean. His love for the island, he told me, made him wish to remain forever, on the knoll of his choice, overlooking the restless sea.

"It will take more than an airfield to change Carriacou," replied Linton reassuringly. "You'll see."

When we climbed by jeep to a peak overlooking Hillsborough Bay, everything was the same except for a few more houses on the outskirts of the town. Palms overhung a double curve of white sand, and the water of the anchorage shaded through pale tones of blue into the azure of the Caribbean. The airfield was only a minor blemish, reminding me of the cow-pasture fields of my early flying days.

As Linton had promised, the Grenadines seemed more firmly wedded to the sea than ever. Although other airstrips are in operation on Palm Island and Mustique,

As day breaks on Mustique, fishermen spread thei

and others will soon follow elsewhere, freight and local passenger traffic still moves by one of the last fleets of commercial sail in existence.

Under the palms of the village of Windward a schooner was taking form, her massive frames hewn from the trunks and branches of cedar trees that provided the curves the shipwrights sought. Above the murmur of wavelets breaking on the sand at her stern rang the thud of ax and adz, the hollow *pung* of caulking mallets.

"We don't use no power tools or plans," I was told by Captain Zepherine McLaren as he rowed me out to the sloop *Mermaid*. Sheltered behind a fringing reef, she seemed set in glass, so clear was the water. "We just goes by shapes in our head and what our eyes tells us."

I stepped on a deck as unyielding as a boulder awash. The mast had been shaped by hand from a balk of timber ten inches

opping nets to dry. Already they have gone out in rowboats to drag their seines in bay shallows.

With leather palm and stout linen thread, a Bequia islander reinforces the edge of a canvas sail.

"A living mariners' museum," the author calls Bequia, where men still go whaling in small boats like the 30-footer above. With harpooners at the bow thwarts, crews begin the chase when lookouts on the hills sight the pluming spouts of their quarry. After a successful hunt,

square. It was supported by rigging made taut with deadeyes and lanyards, as on the vessels of Nelson's day.

"I made even the sails myself," continued the captain. "When she was launched, I said 'Let's go home,' and down she go! On her sailing she have no labor; in a breeze of wind she don't lean."

What Cap'n Zeph did not tell me I had already learned from Linton Rigg. In the 1968 Carriacou Regatta, patterned on the Out Island Regatta in the Bahamas (both inaugurated by Linton), *Mermaid* won her first two races by large margins. On the third day she lay with sails down for ten minutes after the starting gun, "to make things evener," in the words of Cap'n Zeph —then took off after the fleet to win by ten minutes!

At first it seemed strange that a by-product of progress had been a revival of the age of sail. From Grenada to Anguilla I was to see more sloops and schooners than I could remember even from 1947. On St. Vincent my old friend Kenneth Punnett would supply the reason: "The development projects have given them plenty of cargo to haul. Wind is still the cheapest fuel, and here it can be depended upon."

Gone are the camels introduced during the 18th century as beasts of burden, but oddities continue to exist, among them oysters that grow on trees. Overnight we had moved *Sans Terre* from Hillsborough Bay to Tyrrel Bay, and soon after daybreak the next morning young Kitch David and Cuthbert Hamlet rowed us into the Carenage, a quiet inlet that, like many similar ones throughout the Caribbean, owes its name to the practice of careening sailing ships in such protected waters.

"Have people eaten all the oysters?" I asked Kitch jokingly.

"No, sah! Plenty, plen-n-ty oysters, sah."

TED SPIEGEL, RAPHO GUILLUMETTE

all the islanders share the catch. The whalers at right load a harpoon gun they sometimes use, though most prefer to "dart the iron" by hand.

Lifting submerged branches of mangrove trees that stand in the shallow salt water, the boys harvested the heavy encrustation by pulling off the larger shells with their hands. Before, entire branches had been hacked away with a cutlass. I was pleased by the practice of conservation — and by the open friendliness of the boys. Their smiles vanished, however, when I ventured to ask a question about obeah. They looked uneasily at each other, and said nothing.

Obeah is a closed subject between islander and visitor. A form of magic and sorcery not unlike Haiti's more-publicized voodoo, obeah exists in some form on all islands with an African heritage. On Carriacou this heritage is especially strong.

"We have descendants of the Ibo, Moko, Temne, Mandinka, Chamba, and Kromanti tribes," I had been told by District Officer Wilfred A. Redhead on my previous visit. "Their ancestors were brought from Africa more than two centuries ago, but there isn't a man who doesn't know what 'nation' he belongs to."

In a study entitled *Kinship and Community in Carriacou*, published by the Yale University Press in 1962, anthropologist Michael G. Smith wrote of " 'dealers,' who sell human souls to the Devil, and 'door-openers,' whose spells allow them to enter where they will." In island lore there are loup-garous, werewolves that assume different forms to drink the blood of their victims. Generally the loup-garou flies and swoops like a bat, but sometimes it rolls along the ground as a ball of fire. The female counterparts of loup-garous are witches who roam at night looking for sleeping victims, especially fat tender babies. *Diablesses*, cloven-hoofed beauties lurking on uninhabited cays and rocks like the Sirens of Homer's *Odyssey*, destroy the

33

sailors they enchant by driving them mad.

Obeah is a phase of local life that goes on below the surface, sometimes accounting for behavior puzzling to an unsuspecting outsider. Once I had a maid who would not carry salt to the table, and I've heard of cases when healthy people sickened and died for no known medical reason. Local legend tells of a schooner sent to sea without an obeah doctor's blessing: On her maiden voyage she hit a reef and sank.

From the deck of *Mermaid* I looked across a narrow channel to Petit St. Vincent, uninhabited in 1947. When I crossed next day in *Sans Terre*, I found an island symbolizing the new Caribbean. Anchoring where *Carib* had swung alone, we lay among a fleet of visiting charter yachts. Going ashore, I again found a tropic paradise, but of a wholly different character. Twenty-two cottages nestled in carefully

tended shrubbery, and that night I dined on New York-cut sirloin steak served by uniformed waiters on a candle-lit terrace.

The transition is fairly typical of what is happening throughout the Caribbean. Change is inevitable when so many dwellers of northern climes have the time and money to escape winter, and jets make it quick and easy. Everywhere I heard the word "development." As used in the islands, it means the purchase of an islet or tract of land, usually by outside interests. Either a hotel is built or the land cut up into smaller parcels. Roads are laid, and houses built for sale or for rent. What had existed unchanged for centuries is transformed virtually overnight. Nothing else is altering the appearance of the islands so fast, or their economy, or the islanders' outlook on life.

Petit St. Vincent came into being as a

Careened for caulking in Admiralty Bay on the leeward coast of Bequia, a sloop lies on her beam end

resort after industrialist H. W. Nichols, Jr., of Cincinnati sailed in aboard the charter yacht *Jacinta* during the spring of 1965. He found the islet as I had in 1947, still uninhabited, and was enchanted. Buying it from the owner took a full year, and another two years went into constructing the cottages, roads, dining room, laundry, kitchen, generating plant, maintenance shops, and the myriad other things necessary to convert a desert isle into a resort. Because of insufficient rainfall and a lack of wells, it was even necessary to provide drinking water, so a solar still capable of producing 2,000 gallons a day was built.

As the master of a small ship I was staggered by the logistical problems. "Every nut and bolt had to come in by schooner," assistant manager Dave Corrigan told me. "All the materials we had here were stone and sand." Dave had been the mate of *Jacinta;* the captain, Hazen Richardson, became manager, thus preserving the chain of command. Together they had brought a dream to reality.

Near Petit St. Vincent is Palm Island, its name changed from Prune Island as a result of owner John Caldwell's penchant for planting coconut palms everywhere he went as a charter-boat skipper. John and Mary Caldwell came to the Grenadines in 1961 aboard the schooner *Outward Bound,* planning a brief stopover before continuing a voyage around the world. They got no farther. In 1966 they scraped together their savings to take over "the few goats and tangle of weeds" that was Prune. Now they have a hotel consisting of ten duplex cottages and a central dining room-lounge. The remaining land was subdivided into 50 lots; 40 had been sold at the time of my visit, with 11 houses already standing.

While I was impressed by the opportunities the new developments gave nonsailors to savor remote islands in the sun, I confess being happy to steal into the lee of the outermost of the Tobago Cays, a cluster of uninhabited jewels scattered on the velvet of a lagoon formed by a barrier reef. From the flying bridge nothing seemed to

heaved down in the shallows with block and tackle.

lie between *Sans Terre* and the open sea, but to my ears came a distant roaring, and on looking through binoculars I could see Atlantic swells lifting, cresting, then thundering down upon hidden reefs.

As at a Pacific atoll, the water lay calm within embracing arms of coral. Lowering the dinghy from our stern davits, Alvie and I explored the lagoon. Donning mask and snorkel, I chased a grouper into a cavern bracketed by sea fans waving in the current, but had to settle for a mess of lambis, the mollusk called conch in other parts of the West Indies. Later we walked beaches that seemed as remote as Robinson Crusoe's. Although the Tobago Cays have become a favorite rendezvous of the charter fleet, we were alone.

After heading north for Bequia I could not resist stopping at Mustique. On my 1965 cruise I had hesitated to intrude,

knowing it was maintained as a plantation and private domain of Scotsman Colin Tennant. But since I had heard that it, too, was to be developed, I landed on a beach backed by a magnificent stand of palms. Climbing the hill beyond, I saw cattle and horses grazing in a valley bordered by fields of Sea Island cotton and pigeon peas and groves of limes, oranges, and grapefruit.

By chance I met Colin Tennant strolling toward the beach. "Although we'll have an airstrip in the valley," he told me, "we expect to preserve the pastoral quality by continuing agriculture. Initial building will take place on points of land jutting into the sea, and in the groves behind the beaches."

Mustique, covering some 1,300 acres, is larger than the other islands being developed into resorts. As Colin Tennant drove me around in a pint-size English car called a Mini-Moke, he explained that different

Frenzy of the dance whips the skirt of a Carriacouan while a drummer moans to the beat, his face contorted with emotion. One of several Big Drum dances performed for such occasions as marriages and boat launchings, the Belair enlivens a celebration after a day of feasting. Some islanders, following ancestral ways, practice obeah, sorcery similar to the famed voodoo of Haiti.

NATIONAL GEOGRAPHIC PHOTOGRAPHER DEAN CONGER

communities would offer houses of varying price. He even envisioned a cluster of cottages from which boatowners could look down on their yachts in a marina below. Yet despite the scope of the project the island would not become crowded, he assured me. Large areas would remain undeveloped. Perhaps it was this peaceful setting that attracted Princess Margaret, who is among those owning a building site.

My head swirling with thoughts of such a transformation, I came to Bequia, most northerly of the Grenadines. Like Carriacou, it is little affected by change. In the shade of almond trees sailmakers still plied leather palm and needle on canvas and still tarred their hemp. A sloop lay in shallows off Port Elizabeth, careened for repair with tackles fixed to her masthead. Shipwrights swung adzes, forming natural-crook frames in a way unchanged since the

colonial era. Bequia, as before, struck me as a living mariners' museum.

Fittingly, it remains one of the few places in the world where men still pursue and capture whales in small boats. On the beach of Friendship Bay whaleboats awaited the lookout's call, lovely double-ended craft straight from the golden age of Nantucket, complete to the old-time cutout in the bow thwart to steady the harpooner's knee. In a nearby long house roofed with palm thatch, oars and harpoons were stacked. Coiled line lay in tubs, ready for running.

Athneal Ollivierre, chief harpooner and dean of Bequia whalers, told me the 1969 season was the best since he began whaling 29 years ago. The only one of four brothers of French ancestry still active, Athneal is a tall lean man with large powerful hands. As we talked, his eyes roved the dancing offshore waters.

After my 1965 visit their luck was poor, he said. They had not taken a whale until 1968, when they got a small humpback. But in 1969 they had taken six.

The whalers go six to a boat, in as many as four craft. Athneal "darts the iron" by hand, and a bomb is used to finish the harpooned whale. The kill made, the men cut a hole over the nostril and tie a line to keep the mouth closed. If a dead whale fills with water, it will go down, taking the boat with it. The men tow the whales to nearby Petit Nevis, where they render the oil and dry the meat.

The next day I visited Petit Nevis. Approaching from leeward, we could smell it coming. There is nothing quite like the aroma of a whale factory—an odor that seems to permeate, an odor you taste. There is no getting rid of it. Stepping over giant bones and strips of baleen, we picked our way up a slippery concrete ramp to the try-house, where whale oil is rendered in iron caldrons. Exposed to the sun on a hillside above were slabs of drying meat. Thomas G. Johnston, who has a great interest in whaling, told me that although meat was in demand, the oil was not. After the lean years, 30 barrels now awaited a buyer, a disappointing climax.

Whale bones from past catches form part of the decorative motif of Moonhole, Tom Johnston's house, built under a natural stone arch that not only shelters it from sun and rain, but also frames what must be the world's largest picture window. The name Moonhole stems from the way light shining through the opening in the narrow neck of land sometimes resembles a full moon.

Tom Johnston came to Bequia after 25 years as an advertising executive. One Monday morning in New York he awakened "fed up with existing simply for a better job and bigger bank account," so with his wife Gladys he left for the tropics. Intrigued by the natural arch, they began a house which grew stone by stone, taking its inspiration from the setting.

"None of our rooms has more than three walls," Tom reminded me. "Our guest room has only one wall of masonry, to hang a door for privacy. Its sides are the rock of the cliff, the arch overhead is the ceiling—and in front there is only a view."

For friends, Tom was building other houses, all free in form, simple and unembellished except for gifts from the sea. On my previous visit, as I was leaving, Tom had offered to build me a room if I wished to return and there was no space in his home. This time he offered a whole house. When I pointed down to my home afloat, he grinned impishly. The smell of Petit Nevis still perfumed our clothes. "Then stay for dinner," he said hospitably. "I'll cook you a nice whale steak."

NATIONAL GEOGRAPHIC PHOTOGRAPHER WINFIELD PARKS

"More a way of life than it is a home," retired advertising executives Thomas G. Johnston and his wife, Gladys, say of Moonhole, their Bequia refuge. Fitted to the cliff beneath a vault of rock, the multi-level house has thirteen free-form rooms. For cruising and transportation, the Johnstons maintain a small fleet of their own— a 33-foot ketch, three whaleboats, and three dinghies—usually moored in a cove on the other side of Moonhole's narrow neck of land.

TED SPIEGEL, RAPHO GUILLUMETTE

III *St. Vincent:*
The Planter Isle

Palms crowd the sea on St. Vincent, island "horn of plenty" that pours forth a rich bounty of coconuts

O N FIRST VIEW St. Vincent is an island of voluptuous curves swathed in tones of green. "It's like a park, a garden!" exclaimed Alvie Daniels beside me at the wheel. From every wave crest the pattern of cultivated fields became more pronounced, tier on tier from shore to cloud line. Some islands are forbidding from the sea, but St. Vincent might be what a sailor of yore would dream about during a long passage.

Yet it is a haven rarely achieved without a final slap from Neptune. Bequia Channel is notoriously rough. For three thousand miles the trade winds have blown uninterrupted across the Atlantic, generating long rolling seas and a surface drift.

Compressed into the four-mile channel between Bequia and St. Vincent, where the bottom lies only some 200 fathoms deep, the seas rush through in a great trough of turbulent water. The same drift funnels into other passages between islands, continuing across the Caribbean until it causes a mighty piling up on the Central American coast. This mass of water, seeking a normal level, escapes between Cuba and Yucatán, thus giving rise to the Gulf Stream.

We came to anchor in the lee of Young's Island, where we would have better shelter than in the roadstead of Kingstown. Soon, with Kenneth Punnett as my guide, I was seeing the island from a different perspective. Driving up the mountain slopes, I

ananas, Sea Island cotton, and arrowroot. Horses bred for racing graze a deep carpet of pangola grass.

41

"Like George, with courage dauntless, We may all our foes subdue," sing devout marchers on St. George's Day, April 23. In Kingstown, capital of St. Vincent, scouts (right) step to the tempo of the Royal Police Force band as an Anglican procession honors the patron saint of England. Above, white lace frames the faces of young rural girls in town for the festivities.

looked down on the valleys of Greathead and Mesopotamia, tropical horns of plenty that widened and deepened as they spilled toward the sea that would carry their produce to North America and Great Britain. Terraced hillsides and small, carefully tended farm plots alternated with large estates. As before, St. Vincent typified for me the true planter isle.

I could not have had a better guide than Ken, a member of one of the oldest families on the island, settlers "since the days we fought the Caribs and the French."

Through Ken I had come to know Buccament Valley, locally called Punnett Valley. Five members of the family dwell on its slopes in rambling houses, surrounded by lands which give them their heritage and their livelihood. From the lawn of Cane Grove Estate I looked out on pastures of pangola grass that had been a sea of green banana plants when I visited in 1965.

"We've switched to cattle-raising here," said John Punnett, owner of Cane Grove, "but bananas are still the island's principal export. Once, the mainstay was sugarcane —which gave the estate its name—but sugar production became unprofitable in the 1930's because of labor difficulties and outside competition. After that the chief crop was arrowroot; then in 1954 the price of bananas went so high they were known as 'green gold.' Planters converted their fields, and the export of arrowroot slipped from 50,000 barrels to 30,000 by 1962. During the shortage, American manufacturers, our biggest customers, shifted to cornstarch as a substitute for arrowroot."

I learned from Ronald Roach, then general manager of the St. Vincent Co-operative Arrowroot Association, that by 1967 production had dropped to 17,344 barrels and was still declining, partly because bananas continued to be more profitable.

Thus green gold is the dominant factor in island life. Before the weekly "banana ship day," when cargo is loaded into trim white refrigerated ships, antlike processions descend the slopes. Stems heavy with the fruit are cut and carried atop heads to

PAINTING BY HEINRICH BERANN

"The true planter isle," author Mitchell calls volcano-crowned St. Vincent. Fields and forests clothe its slopes from shoreline to summits.

Sails snugly furled, a ketch lingers in Cumberlan

roadside depots. Trucks come along, and bananas and field workers alike ride into Kingstown, the fruit inside, the humans wherever space allows.

From John Punnett I had already learned much about the cultivation of the fruit. "There are many special terms in banana culture," he had told me on my previous visit. "The original bearing plant is called the 'mother.' After reaping, it is cut down, and a new trunk, known as a ratoon or 'follower,' grows from the roots. There can be several ratoons, but here at Cane Grove Estate we plow up the field and replant after the third."

Stopping at a plant bearing an unusually large stem, he showed me the clusters called hands. Each banana is a finger. "Planting in rows spaced 8 feet by 4 feet allows 1,360 plants to the acre," he said. It was a staggering statistic. I visualized whole valleys brimming with the waving leaves and budding stems of green banana plants.

Four years earlier, on neighboring St. Lucia, Sir Garnet Gordon, chairman of the board of Geest Industries (W.I.), Ltd., had furnished me with even more staggering statistics. In 1964 Geest ships carried to the British Isles almost 12 million stems, each averaging 120 fingers. This time I found that the 1969 crop would come to some 15 million stems, or close to two billion ba-

nanas! This represented the yield from Grenada, St. Vincent, St. Lucia, and Dominica alone, without counting Martinique and Guadeloupe, whose crops go to France.

In 1968, fully 70 percent of the revenue of St. Vincent came from banana exports. On Grenada, more diversified through the production of spices, bananas still represented 55 percent of island revenue. Dominica, despite some export of citrus, nevertheless was 75 percent dependent on the one crop, and on St. Lucia green gold represented 85 percent of total revenue.

Government leaders and the public alike are aware of the need to develop additional income sources for these emerging states. The most obvious possibility is tourism, but efforts also are being made to attract industry. As I strolled across Market Square in Kingstown I talked with Desmond Robinson, whom Ken Punnett had dispatched

ay. Here amid the palms islanders greet visiting yachts with the beat of steel drums made from barrels.

to help me in getting a local driver's license.

Desmond and I walked past evidence of the island's simple economy. Women sat on the edge of the sidewalk bordering the square behind baskets of tamarinds and peanuts, limes and charcoal, pawpaws and carrots. Small booths along the waterfront were crammed with household needs from soap to whale meat—Kingstown's markets were running big specials on choice cuts of Bequia whale, my nose had already told me.

I asked Desmond what he considered the greatest change in the island during his lifetime. He answered without hesitation, "Our Deep Water Harbour. Now ships can come alongside to load cargo, and we gets cruise ships, too." Because of improved facilities, cruise ships are making Kingstown a port of call. Before we parted, Desmond added: "De people happy. But de money a little bit tight. We still need factories."

If industry does come, the Deep Water Pier—sometimes referred to as the Deep Water Harbour, although there have been no changes in the port itself—would certainly have helped attract it by providing better port facilities. Ships of 30-foot draught can load cargo directly from a berth 900 feet long. Bananas and other produce move from truck to shed to ship on conveyor belts.

The pier was 80 percent financed by the Canadian government; the local government provided the balance. As one acquaintance put it, "The Canadians furnished the equipment, the engineering know-how, and the cement; we added the labor and the sand."

Throughout the former British colonies I found Canadians financing similar developments. C. F. M. Davis, Kingstown manager of the Canadian Imperial Bank

45

Late afternoon sun lengthens shadows on terraced Dorsetshire
Hill above Kingstown, where in 1793 Capt. William Bligh put
ashore the island's first breadfruit saplings. Other plantings followed,
and today the "free-lunch" trees shade many island dwellings.

Rolling surf and driftwood divert island children innocent of bathing suits. On Biabou Beach (right) a girl roves a scalloped stretch of volcanic sand. Miles of such beaches beckon increasing thousands of visitors to St. Vincent.

The colonists confined the surviving Caribs to a reservation on the flanks of Soufrière, a volcano at the northern end of the island, and forced the chiefs to sign a document stating: "We . . . do swear . . . that we will bear true allegiance to his Majesty George the Third . . . that his said Majesty is rightful Lord and Sovereign of all the island of St. Vincent, and that the lands held by us the Charaibes, are granted through his Majesty's clemency."

To commemorate the event, a silver medal was struck showing Britannia presenting an olive branch to a naked Carib, with the inscription "Peace and Prosperity to St. Vincent." Such was the early march of empire. Now a chapter of history was ending; in 1969 St. Vincent changed status from British colony to Associated State, which puts full independence within reach.

Because of its fertility St. Vincent was chosen in 1765 as the site of the first botanic garden in the Western Hemisphere. One purpose was to introduce exotic and commercial plants from the Far East to the West Indies. In the garden thrives a historic plant.

"This breadfruit grew from a sapling brought to St. Vincent by Capt. William Bligh," I was told by the agricultural officer in charge of the garden, Conrad de Freitas, the first time I had seen the tree. "Bligh sailed on the *Bounty* to introduce breadfruit from the Pacific to these islands. Planters wanted it as food for their slaves.

"When the project failed because of the *Bounty* mutiny, Bligh was sent again in command of H.M.S. *Providence*. This time all went well. Bligh anchored off Kingstown on January 23, 1793, and put ashore 544 plants which had been transported from Tahiti. This is a third-generation 'sucker,' or shoot, from an original root."

The experiment was successful—breadfruit flourishes everywhere in the West Indies. But there was an unforeseen side effect: Why work when lunch grows on trees? Following a daily domestic routine, a woman walks from her door, knocks down a ripe breadfruit with a bamboo pole, and

of Commerce, explained: "Canada's direct connection with the West Indies goes back to the 19th century, to the molasses and codfish trade in Newfoundland schooners. It is through such long association that Canada is interested in the area, and has helped with docks, airport improvements, schools, and medical facilities."

Regardless of developments, the richness of St. Vincent's soil will influence its future, as it has the past. The island's fertile slopes even played a part in the drama of the Caribs. In 1660 the English and the French, in a rare spirit of accord and magnanimity, agreed that St. Vincent should remain in the Indians' possession. But, drawn by the promise of bountiful crops, colonists kept coming. In 1748, through the Treaty of Aix-la-Chapelle, Britain and France reaffirmed a neutral policy toward St. Vincent, St. Lucia, Dominica, and Tobago. The agreement was soon scrapped. Intermittent fighting between Caribs and settlers on St. Vincent turned into full-scale war. A British force finally subdued the Caribs in 1773 after a bloody campaign.

goes back to her cooking fire, while the men snooze in noonday shade.

Again, in my travels about St. Vincent, I was impressed by its beauty and variety. The cultivated terraces running up the Mesopotamia hillsides reminded me of Italy's Riviera. Palm groves flowing down to the leeward beaches, with the roofs of huts showing through, evoked the South Seas. The wild windward coast, where long Atlantic rollers crashed against cliffs topped by scant grass and wind-pruned trees, was straight from the shores of Scotland.

A highlight of my previous visit had been a day spent at Orange Hill Estate. Through heavy sea mist I again glimpsed the town of Argyle, which I guessed might have been named for Argyll by a homesick Scot. Soon, the road became a rutted trail. The earth and beaches looked like packed coal dust as a result of the fallout from Soufrière, whose last eruption in 1902 preceded by one day the disastrous explosion of Mont Pelée on Martinique.

Again I was able to drive across the bed of the Rabacca Dry River, a miniature canyon sliced into Soufrière's flank. After heavy rains, it becomes a raging torrent, cutting off the northeastern corner of St. Vincent for days at a time. This year it was really dry, looking like a gravel pit at the bottom of a coal chute.

Behind this natural moat, Orange Hill continues to exist almost as a feudal community. Four years before, I had been greeted by owner Cyril Barnard. This time he was in England on vacation, and his son Martin conducted me through groves of towering palms where women gathered fallen coconuts into piles for men to husk.

We watched workers seize basketball-size nuts firmly in both hands and slash them down on sharp spikes held between their knees. Within seconds they had removed the tough outer fiber and passed the inner nut along for the next step. In a nearby compound, women chopped the hard spheres neatly in half, allowing the liquid to flow into buckets.

After the women remove the meat from the split shells, it goes into oil-fired driers for 18 hours. It comes out as copra—65

Cloud-scraper volcano, 4,048-foot Soufrière cups a lake on St. Vincent. It last erupted in 190

percent oil—used for soap, shampoo, margarine, and suntan oil. Virtually nothing is wasted. The meal left over after the copra is pressed to remove the oil makes good feed for livestock. Pigs get the coconut milk. Charcoal made from the shell goes into filtering devices.

"Even the outer fiber fills an occasional need," Martin Barnard explained. "We use it as fuel in the old husk-fired furnaces when production is too heavy for our two oil-fired furnaces."

Orange Hill remains almost self-sufficient, with a school, carpenters, masons, and mechanics; it raises its own cattle, poultry, vegetables, and fruit.

Although the estate is the largest producer of coconuts on St. Vincent, with some 120,000 trees yielding a yearly average of

78 nuts each, Martin Barnard has not grown complacent. "We have diversified," he said as we roamed the estate. "Here we have put down 5,000 kola-nut trees, the basis of the cola drinks; they were started in 1968, and should begin to bear in six or seven years. Over there we will plant 50 acres in grapefruit; eventually we may ship some fruit to Britain and can the rest. Over here we have 40 acres in limes, and we plan ultimately to have 200 acres."

Pointing to cattle grazing in the shade of coconut palms, Martin went on to say that beef production was being expanded, with an initial goal of 1,000 pounds of meat a week for the local market. We passed poultry houses whose daily output had already reached 2,000 eggs. But I was most intrigued at hearing of a new market for

...overing the area with ash and killing 2,000 people

Sun-spattered fields lend a hint of the Orient to the fertile valleys south of the ash-fall zone, where careful soil-conservation practices distinguish estates and small farms alike. Near Kingstown, a woman hills a stand of sweet potatoes, piling up soil to protect the roots from the sun.

the estate's staple. "Last year we shipped more than 433,000 coconuts to the United States for sale in groceries and supermarkets," said Martin. Thus the coconuts on display at your grocer's may have come from the trees of Orange Hill.

The air of peace that pervades the estate perhaps stems from the tempo of its groves, for the production of coconuts and other tree fruits cannot be hurried. A palm does not bear until its eighth year, but then lives to a venerable 70. Yet amidst the tranquillity was a mute reminder of the horror of the 1902 eruptions of Soufrière, when 2,000 people perished. Near the copra ovens stood a squat stone building. On my previous visit, Cyril Barnard had told me its grim story.

"When flames began to shoot from the crater, some 40 people crowded into the cellar, which had only one door and a small window. They were the only survivors on the estate. The manager and his wife, who were Scots, were among them at first, but couldn't stand the heat and the smell, so they left and ran toward their house. Two days later they were found dead on the steps."

Soufrière's heat charred trees and plants at Orange Hill. It blighted crops, roasted

51

cattle where they fell, and even overpowered birds on the wing. On the slopes to the north the lands once deeded to the Caribs suffered even more, but most of the Indians were spared. Because of a revolt, practically all of them had been banished to the island of Roatán off the northern coast of Honduras.

On leaving Martin Barnard I paused to talk with a planter of a different ilk. Ezekial Marksman had stopped to rest his donkey in the shade after crossing the Rabacca Dry River. I came upon him sitting comfortably slumped in a saddle hewn from tree branches. A tin pail holding his lunch hung from the pommel. Astern, on the donkey's rump, a grandson lolled on a folded sack.

"We's goin' to my land," explained Ezekial. With the tip of his cutlass he pushed back the brim of his straw hat, then used the blade to point ahead. The West Indian's cutlass, a multi-purpose tool whose name is a reminder of pirate days, is almost a natural extension of his arm.

Ezekial told me he had a farm of five acres, beyond Orange Hill. His crops were "bananas and arrowroot, but not too much arrowroot now because de price not so good." I found him typical of other small landowners: proud, independent, courteous. Carefully tended plots, contributing to the garden aspect of St. Vincent, are proof of their diligence.

BEFORE LEAVING our anchorage I had lunch at Young's Island. Its owner and creator, John W. Houser, believes "buildings should be understated, planting emphasized." Thus I had hardly been aware that the island had been developed into a hotel. Tropic foliage hid cottages, and flowering trees veiled the dining room.

Later, Mr. Houser and I climbed to the top of fortified Duvernette Islet on steps he had restored "so visitors can see what the old fortresses were like." There silent cannon guarded every approach as though still awaiting attack by white-winged fleet or roving pirate.

As I cruised along St. Vincent's west coast to Chateaubelair, each valley and hillside showed the result of care going back for generations, neatly patterned fields alternating with symmetrical ranks of palms. Yet with every mile the brooding mass of Soufrière loomed higher, a reminder that

all has not been conquered by mankind.

As on my other visits, I found that the bathing-suit salesmen of Chateaubelair made little profit on the junior boys' sizes. Bare brown children romped in the shallows and ran among canoes and nets drying on the beach. Most of the village lay strung along a single street. Houses drowsed in the shade of breadfruit trees, which seemed to grow in every tiny backyard. A roly-poly toddler stared from the doorway of the clinic operated by the Canadian Save the Children Fund. Shops were small and dim. Greetings were casual as we passed other strollers. Dogs snoozed at the roadside. A taxi waited patiently in the shade; its name, Easy Does It, seemed to sum up the general mood.

Beyond Chateaubelair the road ended, and so did the planting. Park gave way to jungle. The summit of Soufrière towers to 4,048 feet, and today it was free of cloud. Flooding sunshine sharply etched every fold and convolution. A sudden impulse prompted me to try to see the Falls of Baleine, rarely visited because there is no easy access except by sea, and the water usually is too rough for a landing.

While Alvie circled in Sans Terre, I went ashore. Underfoot, the beach of small pumice stones crunched like peanut brittle. Two boys materialized out of the bush to help me pull the dinghy clear of the water. Both showed strong evidence of Carib blood in their coloring and high cheekbones. They were so shy I expected them to vanish again, but instead they guided me up a clear rushing stream. Fish darted under boulders as we slithered through the tangle of growth lining the banks.

A final turn, and I looked up through a frame of bamboo. High on the side of Soufrière a ribbon of silver tumbled down an ebon cliff. On both sides the all-pervading green of the primeval forest closed in. Above, the sky was the hard blue of lapis lazuli, patterned by silhouettes of frigate birds riding the updrafts on rigid wings. I could do no more for long minutes than gaze in silence. From such moments memories are spun.

Below palm-tufted heights, Chateaubelair Bay offers yachtsmen a deepwater anchorage, starting point for a stiff climb up Soufrière or an easy run north toward the twin peaks of St. Lucia.

NATIONAL GEOGRAPHIC PHOTOGRAPHER WINFIELD PARKS

IV *St. Lucia:*
Island of Green Gold

Glistening banana ship awaits a December cargo in St. Lucia's Port Castries, the sea-flooded crater o

VIEUX FORT, southern port of entry for St. Lucia, was anything but idyllically quiet. Winches clattered as freighters unloaded construction equipment and materials, and a procession of trucks rumbled inland.

"We're getting ready for the jumbo jets," a customs officer told me as he stamped our documents. "Already, a 750-room hotel, the Halcyon, is being built over by Pointe Sable, handy to nearby Beane Field, and the government is pushing through a mountain road which will cut the driving time to Castries from almost two hours to just 45 minutes."

At the airport I could hardly see what was going on for the dust. Bulldozers and other earth-moving machines appeared and disappeared, working at top speed to extend the runways. I felt there could hardly have been a greater sense of urgency when the first airstrip here was built for wartime patrol.

During World War II, Vieux Fort was the site of a U. S. base, part of the "destroyer deal" arranged by Franklin D. Roosevelt and Winston Churchill. Before the United States entered the war, it provided 50 ships for the British in return for 99-year leases at strategic Caribbean locations. From runways built at Vieux Fort, U. S. planes had roared aloft to keep watch over Martinique and surrounding waters during the years the Vichy government of

n ancient volcano. In a cove across the harbor shine reflected lights from the new homes of Sans Soucis.

TED SPIEGEL, RAPHO GUILLUMETTE (ABOVE), AND NATIONAL GEOGRAPHIC PHOTOGRAPHER JAMES L. STANFIELD

Chartered yachts stand motionless in sun-polished Marigot Harbour, south of Castries. Swinging outward from a palm-shaded beach, a tender returns visitors after a trip ashore. Completely landlocked, this inlet offers shelter for small craft even during the most savage storms; one veteran yachtsman calls it "probably the best hurricane hole in these islands."

Smashing through a long swell, *Sans Terre* displays the drive of her twin 120-horsepower diesels and the sturdiness of her hull. The author planned her interior as "a home afloat."

France collaborated with Nazi Germany.

When the postwar world sprouted wings, the airport, which had been turned over to St. Lucia, became one of the earliest in the Caribbean capable of handling commercial traffic. Now it forms the basis of the island government's plans to vault into the future, as bigger and faster planes unload still more visitors.

Yet such is the nature of the Caribbean in transition that two hours after leaving the bustle of Vieux Fort *Sans Terre* crept into the cathedral hush of Anse des Pitons. To port, the mighty volcanic spire of Petit Piton towered 2,461 feet, rising almost vertically from the sea, while to starboard Gros Piton lifted even higher but not so steeply. I had passed by many times after steering for the twin peaks, but never before had I stopped for the night. Now — after three attempts, for the bottom drops down almost as steeply as the peaks rise above — the anchor held. We ran a line ashore from the stern and made it fast to a palm tree.

After the sun vanished below the horizon, a full moon shafted into the valley, outlining each waving frond. It was a night for ghosts to walk. Nowhere else in the West Indies does the past seem so vivid as on St. Lucia. The European phase of its history begins with the familiar theme of discovery by Columbus, who undoubtedly sighted the island in 1502 on his fourth voyage to the New World. It continues with the English and the French fighting each other and the Caribs, while other land-hungry Europeans lurked in the wings.

In the early 17th century Cardinal Richelieu of France deeded St. Lucia to a West Indies trading company — at about the time Charles I of England included it in a grant of the "Caribees Islands" to the Earl of Carlisle. These acts of generosity with real estate that neither clearly owned did not stop an intrepid Netherlands company from landing and trading there.

The Dutch did not stay. Perhaps they were smoked out in the same fashion as were the English settlers in 1640. The Caribs built fires of dried red pepper plants to windward, creating a primitive gas attack which drove the weeping and gasping invaders back to their ships.

St. Lucia changed hands many times as the European powers fought to gain colonies.

Green gold—bananas by the ton—brings in 85 percent of St. Lucia's total revenue. At left, an islander with a gasoline-powered blower sprays the plants to prevent leaf spot.

Banana "headers" at the west wharf in Port Castries load plastic-wrapped stems of fruit into the hold of a refrigerated ship that will carry the cargo to Britain. Cultivated in Asia from distant antiquity, the banana reached the New World in the wake of Columbus, to become a staple of Caribbean diet and export.

TED SPIEGEL, RAPHO GUILLUMETTE

The struggle reached its climax in the latter part of the 18th century. On these heights and their surrounding waters centered much of the drama bearing directly on the destiny of the 13 Colonies to the north in their War of Independence. Had not a large part of Britain's naval and military strength been pinned down on St. Lucia and neighboring islands, it could have been employed against the forces of George Washington, perhaps with results which would have changed the course of history.

The following day, after mooring *Sans Terre* at a marina in Castries harbor, I climbed Morne Fortune, the most bitterly contested prize of all. Five times in the possession of the French after 1760, five times taken by the British, St. Lucia was a strategic island, and 852-foot-high Morne Fortune, commanding the town and port of Castries, was the key to St. Lucia. On its plunging slopes men died in windrows in many battles, toiling upward through withering enemy fire.

The British 27th Regiment showed such exceptional bravery in storming the heights at bayonet point on May 24, 1796, that the commander honored the regiment by flying its colors over the captured fortress for an hour before hoisting the British flag. The seesaw of attacker and defender went on until 1814, when the island was ceded to Britain for the last time. Morne Fortune became another remnant of bygone glory. Goats grazed among its monuments while the barracks crumbled into ruin.

Now I found the Morne changed almost beyond belief. Houses perched on the

Youthful St. Lucian mends a 400-foot seine trailing from poles that hoist it for drying. Beyond, Petit Piton bulks 2,461 feet high. Boatmen (right) lower a close-meshed net into a long-boat before a day of fishing. St. Lucia's peaceful occupations veil a bitter past—five times in the possession of the French and five times taken by the British between 1760 and 1814.

upper slopes, their terraces open to a panorama of romance and beauty. Masons and carpenters swarmed over barracks and other buildings not yet renovated.

"The people of St. Lucia bought the summit and installations from the British war department in 1962," I was told later by J. Allen Bousquet, Chairman of the Morne Authority, a government agency, "but nothing was undertaken immediately. Now we have divided the area into 316 building lots for homes. A part is set aside for a hotel. The central parade ground and historical sites will be preserved as a park and playing field. Existing buildings, such as former barracks, will be used by government and semi-government institutions."

One of the old barracks has become a teachers' training college. Another is being converted into a technical school. But perhaps the most fitting monuments to the soldiers who perished from tropical diseases—far more deadly in past centuries than Carib arrows or enemy bullets—are the laboratory and research wards that are a cooperative project of the government of St. Lucia and the Rockefeller Foundation.

"Schistosomiasis is one of the great unconquered parasitic diseases," Dr. Peter Jordan said as we sat in his office atop the Morne. "Probably it affects some 200 million human beings throughout the world. It is basically an illness that strikes where sanitation and a piped water supply are lacking. Certain freshwater snails become infected with parasite eggs excreted by humans. The larvae develop in the snail, which then sheds thousands of organisms capable of penetrating the skin of persons using the water or working in irrigated fields.

"The parasite debilitates infected workers and may be an obstacle to increased production of food in many of the countries that need it most.

"Schistosomiasis has been controlled in other countries, but no comparative study

Clutching dolls, girls wait with their mother (right) at Vigie Airport near Castries. In the future, short-haul jets will use Vigie while international traffic and the jumbo jets call at newly extended Beane Field, farther from town.

Almost in unison, children clap hands to the rhythm of a song spinning from a record at St. Joseph's Convent in Castries. Many youngsters speak patois—a mixture of tongues—at home and begin exploring English at sessions like this.

TED SPIEGEL, RAPHO GUILLUMETTE

of control methods has ever been attempted. In St. Lucia three methods are to be tried in separate valleys—mass medical treatment, killing of the snails, and provision of adequate uninfected water."

Dr. Jordan, who is working with 12 others of European extraction and some 50 St. Lucians, estimates it will take about five years to evaluate the results of the tests.

St. Lucia was astir from the airport extension in the south to the residential development of Cap Estate at the northern tip, which I visited with George Eggleston, an American writer who has become part of the island community. Leaving his home in Castries, we drove through the public-housing project of Sans Soucis, across the harbor from the capital. Homes had begun to rise even as bulldozers filled low land. Designed by the United Nations Physical Planning Office to ease the housing shortage, the project will include shops and a harbor for fishing boats.

On my 1965 visit George had told me about the rise in land values. Back in the 1920's and '30's, the government was eager to dispose of uncultivated land to settlers. "They asked from 10 to 20 shillings an acre —about $2.50 to $5.00 then," he had said. "Even when you were here in *Carib* you could probably have bought all the land surrounding Marigot Harbour for $1,500."

In 1965 one small area facing Marigot Harbour had been subdivided into 226 one-third-acre lots having an average price of $5,000, which added up to $1,130,000. Now when I asked George the price, he suggested I go directly to the office of Marigot Development Limited.

"The average price of our lots is now approximately $7,500," I was told by Mrs. Shirley Spicer. "Over half are already sold. When people used to come in, I'd say, 'Go home and think it over.' Today things are

moving so fast I say, 'You had better do something soon or the lot you want may not be here when you get back.'"

Yet despite the increasingly new look, St. Lucia remains a planter isle. In a population of 115,000, there are 16,400 banana growers registered with the cooperative association that controls sales. "Banana ship day" is an event extending to remote fastnesses, where sheds serve as roadside pickup stations. Geest Industries, Ltd., whose sleek white ships transport the crop to Britain, has a rule that no more than 36 hours can elapse between cutting a stem and loading it into a refrigerated cargo hold. Thus when a vessel warps alongside the Castries wharf and throws open the loading doors, the pace is frantic.

I watched lines of women form in an adjoining warehouse to meet lines of banana-laden trucks winding down the hillsides. A procession began which reminded me of worker ants hurrying to empty an oversize sugar bowl. Balancing a plastic-sheathed stem of bananas on her head, each woman set off almost at a run for the ship, passing

65

another line streaming back for a new load.

"The women load 1,100 to 1,400 stems per door per hour, and we usually work four or five doors at a time," a Geest official told me, shouting above the din. "In two six-hour shifts they will carry on their heads 1,000 tons of bananas. The work is hard, but 'headers' can make more in a few hours than they can on a plantation in a week. They resist change—they don't want the loading facilities mechanized because that would mean the loss of their jobs."

Elsewhere Castries has a modern air. In 1948 a disastrous fire destroyed four-fifths of the city. A second fire in 1951, not so serious, destroyed many dwellings. Since its rebuilding, Castries looks more like a town in Florida than one in the Windward Islands. Glass-fronted department stores have replaced dim shops; banks and other buildings are of contemporary design.

From Sydney Bagshaw, an American artist who came to St. Lucia to retire, and now finds himself with "a business getting out of hand," I learned more about the tourist boom. "In the 1967-68 winter season, 38 cruise ships and 745 yachts called," he told me. "During the next season, the fleet grew to 102 cruise ships and more than 1,000 yachts."

Mr. Bagshaw and his wife arrived in 1961 and began silk-screen printing of fabric to keep themselves busy. Two years later, the local Red Cross asked them to design some women's clothes for a fashion show. "We made up a few dresses—our first—and displayed some prints. Passengers from the next cruise ship bought the lot. We couldn't make dresses fast enough, so we began selling sew-it-yourself kits—front and back panels, plus enough material for sleeves. Thus the ladies can have an original floral, fish, bird, or other design by us, plus their own styling. Now 75 percent of our business is in the kits."

An automobile expedition along the coastal road to the south soon showed the other side of island life. After passing through a sea of banana plants in the valley beyond Morne Fortune, the road snaked around hillsides hanging over the Caribbean until it reached the town of Soufrière, snuggled under the shoulders of Petit Piton. There fishermen hauled nets into narrow dugout canoes as children splashed in the shallows. Pigs, goats, chickens, and sheep foraged behind the beach.

Beyond the town, climbing again, the road entered a forest of towering bamboo and giant fern, then abruptly came to a

TED SPIEGEL, RAPHO GUILLUMETTE

Heading homeward after a hunt for dolphin and kingfish, fishermen hope their boat lives up to its name. Local lore says the cleaverlike bow of their pirogue resembles the rams of Carib war canoes. Spray-lashed boatmen ride out a squall off St. Lucia's southern tip (right).

volcanically blighted area where not even a blade of grass survived. St. Lucia, like its volcanic neighbors, has its Soufrière, which stems from the French *soufre,* meaning "sulphur." Here the mighty forces that lifted the peaks above the sea were still at work. Over witches' caldrons of black water and mud hung a mist pungent with the rotten-egg smell of sulphur. Picking my way along crater rims which grew hotter as the slopes rose, I finally stood staring into a pit of bubbling yellow, barely visible through swirling clouds of reeking steam.

Nearby were springs whose curative powers so impressed the doctors of Louis XVI that bathhouses were built for the French troops in 1784. While the waters of Soufrière effected no miraculous cures, in an era when neither malaria nor yellow fever had been traced to the mosquito, they probably comforted soldiers suffering from skin irritations caused by heat and insects.

Undoubtedly British soldiers used the same baths when their turn came. All over the island are reminders of the duality of St. Lucia's past. On Morne Fortune, the ruined barracks and other buildings testify to the frequent change in masters. The French built of stone, the British of brick. There were buildings of each, and a few of both, where the engineers of one completed a job begun by the other.

The blending of cultures is equally apparent in food and place-names. Gallic herbs and sauces enliven the simplest island dishes, and maps show Londonderry as a village in the hills behind Anse de la Rivière Dorée, while Pigeon Island lies across from Gros Islet.

MORE SURPRISING was an encounter on the road between Soufrière and Vieux Fort. I drove so far through a forest without seeing a wayside hut that I wondered if I had lost my way. Finally I came upon a woman trudging along with a stem of bananas on her head. Asking directions, I found she could speak no English. On an island that had been part of the British Empire for a century and a half, her only language was a patois, a mixture of a few Carib and African words on a French base. When I repeated my question in French, we could converse haltingly.

Returning to Castries along the windward coast, I drove past broad, sloping fields where cattle grazed, and lowlands once planted in sugarcane. Then the road swooped upward over spurs jutting from the central spine. The towns of Micoud and Dennery huddled in deep semiprotected coves where Atlantic surf creamed almost to the doorsteps of the houses. Crossing the cool mountain roof, I looked down once again into the port of Castries.

So celebrated are battles ashore that the part played by the warring navies is sometimes overlooked. Yet the struggle for supremacy in the West Indies took place during days when sea power, at once the sword and buckler of island peoples, was the deciding factor in colonial affairs. And rarely in its history had the naval might of England begun a more dramatic or momentous operation than from the shores of St. Lucia. As *Sans Terre* came to anchor off Pigeon Island, after crossing Gros Islet Bay on the way from Castries, I had the same feeling of association with history that I experienced atop Morne Fortune.

From a lookout tower on the summit of Pigeon Island, Admiral Sir George Rodney had kept watch for long weeks in 1782. In the bay behind, the British fleet lay waiting. Across a 20-mile gap of water was Martinique. Under the shelter of shore batteries in Fort Royal, now Fort de France, rival Admiral Comte de Grasse prepared the French fleet for a rendezvous with Spanish ships off the north coast of Hispaniola. If they could join forces, the British would be overwhelmingly outnumbered.

Then, at dawn on April 8, a swift picket vessel brought word that De Grasse had sailed from Fort Royal. Looking down from the stone tower where Rodney had paced, brass telescope in hand, I could visualize the scene: bosun's pipes shrilling, signal flags fluttering, sailors loading ships' cannon while the ponderous yards overhead swung to the breeze, and tough old Admiral Rodney pacing the quarterdeck of his flagship as he took off in pursuit.

Soon *Sans Terre* would follow in the wake of the rival fleets. But first came a swim, lunch on deck, and a siesta. The Caribbees are still isles of mañana.

Reeking vapors swirl above pools of boiling mud and sulphur-laden water on Soufrière, St. Lucia's active volcano. The author steps cautiously toward the caldrons, his camera in hand.

NATIONAL GEOGRAPHIC PHOTOGRAPHER WINFIELD PARKS

V Martinique:
A Touch of France

Gleaming vision of Paris rises above the treetops on a misty hillside at Balata, north of Fort de France

MARTINIQUE has always been, for me, a bit of France that somehow managed to slip its moorings and drift to a tropic sea.

Dropping anchor under the guns of Fort St. Louis, which had stood guard over De Grasse's fleet, I was welcomed by the familiar skyline of Fort de France. High on one of the surrounding hills, in the village of Balata, gleamed the snow-white dome of the church of Sacré Coeur, reminiscent of the Sacré-Coeur of Montmartre, which looks down on Paris.

Ashore, the illusion of being in France was almost complete. Lining streets near the waterfront were boutiques displaying Dior neckties, Hermès scarfs, and Chanel perfumes, much like a miniature of Rue St. Honoré, a chic Parisian shopping street. Gourmet stores offered pâté de foie gras, a vast selection of wines and cheeses, and even such rarities as fresh grapes flown from France.

Sitting in a sidewalk cafe, I was surrounded by chattering couples sipping apéritifs, and lone men hunched over newspapers—*France-Antilles* instead of *France-Soir*, but the atmosphere was the same. It was as though I had made a great error in navigation and ended up in Europe.

Fort de France is often called "the Paris of the Antilles," but to me it is more like

Martinique's church of Sacré Coeur echoes the style and name of the great basilica of Montmartre.

Marseilles, with its busy waterfront and ship-repair yards, its mixed population and hot sunshine, its complex of industry set into a productive countryside, just as the rest of the island has its closest kinship with the part of France that borders upon the Mediterranean.

At first glance, change was less apparent than on islands to the south, but I soon found these impressions were deceptive. Before, Fort de France had seemed a bustling metropolis in comparison to the sleepy colonial capitals. Now that all the islands were on the march, the difference was less apparent, but Martinique, with its 335,000 people, moves swiftly ahead.

"Our consumption of electricity rises at the rate of 17 percent annually," I was told by André Garcin, director of Crédit Martiniquais, one of the island's leading banks. "In the past ten years the number of telephones has gone from less than 3,000 to more than 10,000. In 1965 there were 114 first-class hotel rooms available; by the end

H.M.S. *Diamond Rock* — in 1804, with Britain and France at war, the Rock southwest of Martinique became a bastion of the British fleet and a commissioned sloop of war. From its sheer heights, 120 sailors-turned-mountaineers cannonaded French ships running the blockade of Fort de France. In this contemporary engraving, defenders hoist provisions to the garrison on the Rock, still saluted by British Navy vessels.

Mountainous Martinique lies halfway between Dominica and St. Lucia. Its people speak Creole, a patois, and French, the official language.

PAINTING BY HEINRICH BERANN

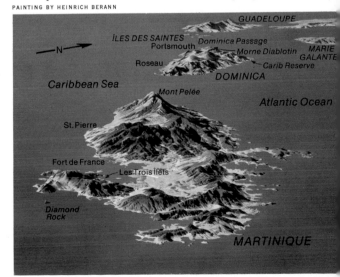

of 1970 there will be more than 900, plus a golf course of championship caliber."

To open additional areas to agriculture, a pipeline has been built from the north of the island, where rainfall is heavy, to the arid west coast. Three broad new *autoroutes* speed traffic. Docks have been expanded and modernized, and an oil refinery is under construction in an area called La Californie, on Fort de France Bay.

As an overseas department of France — comparable to statehood in the United

States—Martinique suffers none of the political growing pains apparent in islands learning to make their way alone. Through three elected representatives in the National Assembly in Paris, it has since 1946 enjoyed a voice in the affairs of the Republic. Arguments in cafes turned more on issues in Paris than on local politics.

Yet Martinique has an ambience all its own, a beat, a flavor as different from continental France as from its British neighbors. Much of the difference stems from an unselfconscious blending of the Gallic and the African, producing a unique culture and people. The exuberant spirit of the Martiniquais finds outlet in the beguine, a dance popularized throughout the world by Cole Porter. It also finds expression in the colorful costumes worn by Creole belles at the time of Carnival, and sometimes on Sundays and holidays.

At the turn of the century author Lafcadio Hearn described the islanders as "fantastic, astonishing—a population of the Arabian Nights." He was especially intrigued by the women's characteristic headdress, "an immense Madras handkerchief, which is folded about the head with admirable art, like a turban;—one bright end . . . being left sticking up like a plume."

The madras headdresses are often seen, but with an innovation since the days of Hearn. As many as four points are left protruding. Having heard conflicting stories about the meaning of the number of points, I asked Mme Yvonne Calvert to set me straight. Long an associate of Groupe Folklorique Martiniquais, organized to preserve folk dances, she is an expert on the customs of the island.

"One point signifies 'My heart is free—I'm looking for a friend,'" she replied. "Two points mean 'I am promised; you are wasting your time.' Three points, 'Don't bother me—I'm happily married.' But four points signal, 'I'm not exactly free, but there is room in my life for one more.'"

It is during the season of Carnival that the spirit of the Martiniquais finds its fullest expression, in a mad swirl of gaiety. "Here Carnival goes on for six weeks," Mme Calvert continued. "Each Sunday there is a different theme for the maskers. One week it may be 'Martinique in her native dress,' when even little girls wear the full skirts, the foulard, and the pointed madras

Les Martiniquaises: Above, girls in traditional embroidered blouses and rippling skirts dance for passengers on the French Line cruise ship *Flandre,* moored at Fort de France, capital of Martinique. Tied to display a single point, the madras kerchief signifies "My heart is free." Costumed dolls, often bought by visitors for little girls back home, offer varying styles; a snoozing child enjoys a dream brighter than fashion.

headdress. Another week we may have 'Pierrot and Pierrette' clown costumes.

"On other islands, Mardi Gras is the climax, the end of Carnival, but on Martinique, it goes on through Ash Wednesday, and the last day is unique. Everybody dresses in black-and-white costumes, mourning King Carnival, who is to die in a few hours. He is carried in effigy through the streets and burned at dusk in the waterfront park or on a barge anchored offshore. But the merrymaking goes on until midnight, with the crowds singing, '*Vaval pas quitté nous,*' 'Carnival don't leave us.'"

Driving to the village of Fond Marie-Reine on the lower slopes of Mont Pelée, I dined at a tiny restaurant that gave me an insight into rural Martinique by combining true native cuisine with a touch of carnival—in the bright dress and high

spirits of the owner, Mme Joséphine Nirvi. I was accompanied by Philip Silcott, an editor for the National Geographic Society, his wife Marjorie, and their daughter Catherine Sue, age 7.

I had arranged for the meal earlier in the week when I stopped at a display of fruit and found also a kitchen, plus a few tables and chairs, under a thatch roof.

Now we found that the luncheon had become an event in the simple community. Mme Nirvi had donned a bright apron over layers of swirling skirts. Around her neck hung masses of gold chains, and an elaborate coiffure was topped by a colorful madras—discreetly tied into three points.

We were shown to a table in the best room, next to the kitchen, where dogs and chickens wandered. Little Catherine Sue left the table for a few moments to make

Waxy anthuriums bloom in a forest plantation not far from Fort de France. Mme Joseph Bonne, wife of the estate's owner, snips flowers for export to France and West Germany. Her son places them in vials of water before packing.

friends with a caged rabbit. Passers-by paused to stare curiously through the open door—tourists had not yet come in any number to the village. Lunch began with "calalu," a thick soup made from dark green leaves looking like oversize spinach. As at any proper French table, long crackly loaves of bread were passed, and bottles of wine and mineral water stood in ranks.

What made the day most memorable was Mme Nirvi herself. She directed the single waitress with the ceremony of a majordomo overseeing an imperial ball. Eyes flashing, earrings swinging, she replied to our sallies with zest and humor. Watching the aplomb of Mme Nirvi, I could not help thinking of another Joséphine, a Martiniquaise also equal to any occasion.

Marie Rose Joséphine Tascher de la Pagerie, who grew up to become Napoleon's empress, was born at the village of Les Trois Îlets, near Fort de France. One of my favorite places to rest after rambles through Fort de France is a bench in La Savane, the waterfront park, near a statue of Joséphine in her coronation robes. Surrounded by palms rustling in the warm wind, she gazes across the glittering waters of the bay toward her birthplace.

Another reminder of the past redounds to the glory of Great Britain. Off the southwest corner of Martinique lies Diamond Rock. On previous passages I had only sailed past, but this time, in the grip of history, I made a circumnavigation. More than ever Diamond Rock looked to me like

77

a great stone haystack, with almost vertical sides and a rounded summit. Churning currents and breaking seas made approach dangerous, and to climb it seemed a task for mountaineers, not sailors.

In January 1804 Commodore Sir Samuel Hood anchored his flagship *Centaur* as close to the rock as he dared. Months before, a British squadron under his command had imposed a blockade on the French, but Hood found supply ships slipping through the channel between Diamond Rock and Martinique.

To seal the gap, a detachment of sailors climbed to the top and fixed a tackle to a pinnacle. Laboriously the men hoisted five cannon from the ship, looking to a witness like "mice, hauling a little sausage."

For 17 months 120 men and boys under the command of Lt. J. W. Maurice harassed enemy shipping from the heights. Not until June 2, 1805, was the brave band dislodged. A heavily armed French squadron finally captured the position at a loss to themselves of 30 killed, 40 wounded, and three gunboats destroyed, against two men killed and one wounded on the British side.

In commemoration the British accorded the forbidding pinnacle a rare honor — it was commissioned as H.M.S. *Diamond Rock*, a sloop of war. Royal Navy ships still fire a seven-gun salute as they pass.

One escaped: Of St. Pierre's 30,000 people, only Ludger Sylbaris survived — held in solitary confinement in a thick-walled cell. Volcanic ash nearly buries the door.

PAINTING BY PAUL CALLE

May 8, 1902: Incandescent gas and superheated steam explode from Mont Pelée, blacking out the sun and turning the city and harbor of St. Pierre into a flaming caldron. "It was like witnessing the end of the world," said the captain of the steamer *Roddam*, only vessel in the harbor to stay afloat. Officials had assured the people that preliminary mudflows and ashfalls gave no cause for alarm — or for seeking safety elsewhere. Correspondents (right) explore the ruins of Rue Victor Hugo, once the Broadway of a charming colonial city.

Dusk-veiled Mont Pelée broods above the rebuilt city of St. Pierre, now home to only 6,500 people. Joseph Bonnet-Durival (above), former curator of the local museum, holds a bottle fused by heat from the volcano. Moved out of the threatened city by his father when he was 11, he recalls a "dreadful noise," heard hundreds of miles. Pelée erupted at 7:50 in the morning and within three minutes transformed the city into a desert of ash. The watch (below) ticked on for 14 minutes before Pelée stopped it.

Based on my home afloat, anchored off La Savane Park and commuting by dinghy, I was in a good position to savor all sides of island life. Bistros in Fort de France served such continental delicacies as *escargots*, the snails beloved by gourmets; *caneton à l'orange*, duckling roasted with an orange sauce, and for dessert thin *crêpes Suzette* in flaming liqueurs.

Often when wandering back streets I encountered a courtesy described by earlier visitors: When I asked directions, a passerby would accompany me to my destination, answering my thanks with a bow and smiling, "*Pas de quoi, monsieur*," before continuing on his way.

As I watched cruise ships pouring visitors ashore—Martinique is one of the most popular stops on Caribbean winter cruises—every taxi capable of wheezing up a hill converged on the boat landing. Streets quickly filled with visitors wearing fresh sunburns and weird straw hats, mementos of other ports.

On those days the boutiques swirled with confusion, for time is short and French perfumes and kindred items sell at free-port prices. Often among the final sidewalk purchases was a madras kerchief, which the smiling *vendeuse* was happy to tie into a headdress before *madame* went back to the ship. With typical Gallic humor, usually one or four points were left sticking up—always I wondered if the visitor knew what she was signaling in the island code!

Exploring the countryside, I had the opportunity to play a role in a workaday drama I had often witnessed. Under the palms and drying nets of the seaside community of Fond Lahaye, canoes were drawn up on the sand. Leaning against the nearest was Marie-Victoire Anastase, 65, who told me he had been a fisherman all his life.

"Everything has changed but our way of catching fish," he said reflectively, puffing on a pipe. "*Regardez.* You ask how we take them in our village. You will see."

As we watched, a crew slid a fishing

canoe, or *gommier,* into the water, and began paying out a net over the stern. The oarsmen tugged, and the laden craft swung seaward in a long arc. Near us, two men held a rope attached to the net to keep one end in the shallows. Slowly the canoe completed its half-circle, coming back to shore at the opposite end of the village beach.

At first, only two men on each rope began to haul, but gradually they were joined by others drifting out from under the trees: men, women, children—and me. It was too good a chance to miss, and I was accepted as an acquaintance of old Marie-Victoire's.

The rope was of coarse Manila hemp, wire-stiff from caked salt. In unison our line swayed, gaining inches at a time, to the rhythmic chant of *"Viens, viens, viens—* Come, come, come!" From the gommier offshore, Bertrand Merlin, master of the haul, threw stones and splashed the water with a paddle to keep fish from escaping.

Gradually the net shrank from a half-circle to a horseshoe to a hairpin. Finally we had our prey: In bushels of seaweed gleamed perhaps two hundred tiny flapping bits of iridescence—local varieties of sardine, anchovy, and baby mackerel. None seemed bigger than a child might catch on a bent pin, but nothing was overlooked.

Bertrand pawed through mounds of seaweed, selecting the larger fish and tossing the seaweed farther up the beach. Each handful was then sifted by old women and children, who put the minnows they retrieved into coconut shells. Finally the village cats took over the search. No one, I felt, had a prize large enough to match the size of my two blisters.

Despite the *joie de vivre* of Martinique, its former capital, St. Pierre, still lies under the pall of one of the great tragedies of the 20th century. On May 8, 1902, a cloud of incandescent gas and superheated steam burst from Mont Pelée to envelop the town at its base.

Lafcadio Hearn, in *Two Years in the French West Indies,* wrote of St. Pierre in the 1880's as "the quaintest, queerest, and the prettiest withal, among West Indian cities."

Carnival revelers and parading floats throng Fort de France in a pageant lasting from mid-January until midnight on Ash Wednesday. The streets resound with the rhythm of the popular beguine, a dance that originated on Martinique.

NATIONAL GEOGRAPHIC PHOTOGRAPHER WINFIELD PARKS

83

In seconds it was in ruins. Except for one prisoner in a hillside cell, all the people in the city—some 30,000—perished.

As I strolled the streets with the Silcotts, we were impressed by what St. Pierre must have been in its days of glory. Wide double flights of steps led to the foyer of the theater. Ruined walls testified to a spacious interior. Once actors had traveled all the way from France to play before wealthy Creole planter families.

At the museum of St. Pierre, then-curator Joseph Bonnet-Durival, 78, told us about the eruption. The old gentleman was even more bent and fragile than on my last visit, but his cataract-blinded eyes still saw vividly the awesome moment of the past.

"I was 11 years old and remember it well," he said as before, tapping his way between display cases with a cane. "My father had moved us out of town, toward Le Carbet. I saw the cloud of steam coming down toward St. Pierre with a dreadful noise, carrying ashes and stone but no lava, moving with terrific speed.

"The ships in the harbor were overwhelmed and sunk, all except the *Roddam*, which was torn from her anchors and crept to St. Lucia with the news."

M. Bonnet-Durival, who, though blind, knows every cranny of the museum, pointed to grim exhibits in the display cases: nails fused into a blob, a bunch of keys welded into a mass, cinders that once were books or food, the poor box from a church with the coins run together. Afterward, again walking the still-scarred streets, I felt the town contained memories that could never be erased, even by the shouts of children playing among the ruins.

Later, we drove high up Pelée, now green and peaceful under a cap of clouds. An observation station a few miles away keeps watch on the sleeping giant, but volcanologists detect no sign of another nightmare.

On each previous visit to Martinique I had lunched at the 200-year-old mansion of Acajou, the domain of Charles Clément. Sadly, my old friend was too ill to receive visitors himself, but he insisted I come to the house and bring the Silcotts. We were received by three of M. Clément's sons, and a nephew, Maurice Iman.

Acajou has not changed in the quarter-century I have known it. In French the name means "mahogany," and the wide boards of that wood used in building the house have turned silver-gray with age, a lovely contrast to the terrace of faded-rose bricks and the weathered tile roof tinged green with lichens. A jalousied porch surrounds a center room supported by beams —dark and cool, yet open to every stray breeze of summer.

As Cathy Silcott watched a hummingbird flit among vases of cut flowers, Phil and Marjorie had their introduction to a Martinique punch, all ingredients of which were products of the estate: white rum, sugar syrup, and the freshly squeezed juice of small limes. Afterward, we visited the distillery below, where iron rollers crushed stalks of cane. Juice ran through open sluices to ferment in huge vats. As we followed the process past clanking machinery and wheezing stills, I saw a familiar face.

Victor Martinel had worked with M. Clément at Acajou distillery for 38 years, and he remembered my previous visits. A mechanic, Victor keeps the venerable machinery *en marche*. "This steam engine came to Fort de France more than 70 years ago to pump the drydock," he shouted as he caressed a black iron flank. "It works from February to June, when the cane is being cut, and I work the rest of the year getting it ready for the next season, while the other workers rest."

Our final stop with Maurice Iman was a warehouse where rum slumbered in charred barrels, some as long as 15 years. "In colonial days sugarcane was grown as widely among the islands as bananas are today," M. Clément had told me previously, "and almost every estate produced rum, usually as a by-product of molasses. Producing *rhum vieux,* our dark aged rum, is almost exactly the same process as making cognac from the pressing of grapes."

Martinique is an island I leave with regret. Thus I was cheered by André Garcin's farewell. "Remember," he reminded me, "our nickname for Martinique is '*L'Île des Revenants,*' which for us means 'the isle where people come back.' So we'll say *au revoir* and not goodbye."

Petites Pierrettes dress up for Carnival with slight modifications of the costume of a French clown. One adapts the makeup as well—clearcut blotches of rouge. Each Sunday in Carnival brings throngs of merrymakers into the streets.

NATIONAL GEOGRAPHIC PHOTOGRAPHER WINFIELD PARKS

VI *Dominica:*
The Loneliest Isle

Fluted bases of the swamp bloodwood grope in the waters of a virgin forest on Dominica, long th

LOOMING IN THE DISTANCE, Dominica appeared timeless—mountains swathed in green, a mass of vegetation so luxuriant that nature is almost an enemy, an island where man's works in the past were mere scratches. When approaching by sea, I imagine I might be a Carib chief standing in the bow of a canoe, scanning the almost vertical shoreline, so little has it changed through the centuries.

Yet time may be running out for Dominica as a virgin fastness. After anchoring *Sans Terre* in a thick scum of oil spilled in Woodbridge Bay, on the outskirts of the capital city of Roseau, I went ashore to rent a car. As I drove north along the coastal road, I passed hillsides gouged out to har-

vest pumice, which is shipped to the U. S. Virgin Islands for use in the manufacture of lightweight building blocks.

Then I turned to climb the road winding up the Layou River valley. Soon I heard the whine of woodsmen's saws. On both sides of the road lay patches of raw, red earth. I stopped the car to walk through acres of stumps, small trees crushed to the ground, and deep furrows left by bulldozers and tractors dragging logs to waiting trucks.

In 1965 I had talked with Dr. J. F. Gates Clarke, Senior Entomologist of the Smithsonian Institution in Washington, D. C., who was collecting insect specimens for a biological survey. "Dominica is the least

...ast-disturbed of Caribbean isles. Today loggers cut timber—and roads—in the mountainous land.

HIBISCUS (HIBISCUS ARCHERI),
APPROXIMATELY LIFE-SIZE

FALSE CHAMELEON, OR ANOLE
(AMEIVA FUSCATA), 2/3 LIFE-SIZE

Flora and fauna of a wild land: Dominica's dense forests shelter creatures as diverse as the tree-dwelling anole, its throat distended to woo or to warn, and the male Hercules beetle, whose awesome horns serve mainly in clumsy jousting with rivals. When the insect is airborne, seven-inch wings propel it at speeds approaching 50 miles an hour. Claws upraised, a freshwater crab (opposite) glares with periscope eyes, ready for a fight. The giant katydid crouches on a leaf, detecting sounds with sensitive organs in its front legs. A crimson corolla rings pollen-tufted stamens of the hibiscus (above). As many as forty of these radiant flowers blaze on a single bush.

FRED WARD, BLACK STAR

HERCULES BEETLE (DYNASTES HERCULES), LIFE-SIZE

GIANT KATYDID (MASTOPHYLLUM SCABRICOLLE), LIFE-SIZE

FRESHWATER CRAB (GUINOTIA DENTATA), LIFE-SIZE

disturbed of the West Indian islands," he told me. "Tremendous tracts of untouched primeval forest remain here exactly as they were before the coming of Columbus."

It was precisely this which attracted a group of Canadian businessmen.

"Dominica has one of the few accessible virgin forests left in the Western Hemisphere," Wilbur Mattson, logging manager of Dom-Can Timbers, Ltd., said to me in his Roseau office. "We conducted a company survey in 1967 and found that methods of logging and road construction used in British Columbia would apply here. The lack of snow is made up for by the rain and mud."

Shortly after Dominica became an Associated State in 1967, Dom-Can reached an agreement with the government to cut timber, including such fine hardwood trees as mahogany and gommier, on Crown lands, which comprise approximately a third of the island. It is estimated that over the 21 years of the agreement the yield will exceed one billion board feet of timber. In addition Dom-Can has negotiated with individual owners to cut private lands.

A prefabricated mill with an annual capacity of 12 million board feet was shipped from Canada and assembled in April 1968, and timbering began in July. I confess a feeling of sadness as I looked at the map in Mr. Mattson's office showing the areas that eventually would come under the bite of chain saws. In the Layou Valley, roads are being extended at the rate of 200 feet a day. What I had thought impossible—the penetration of Dominica's seemingly impenetrable forests—goes on apace.

Certainly a visitor would prefer that Dominica retain its pristine beauty, but Mr. Mattson explained his side of the operation: "We have begun to replant cleared areas; we are planning on the basis of a sustained yield—meaning that new timber will be ready before the old is logged off. Large areas will be left intact as preserves. And we are helping to create the jobs Dominica needs so badly in its economy.

"Within two years we expect to have 400

Emerald Pool waterfall spills into a secluded forest glade draped with lianas and ferns. Stems of sun-flamed heliconia arch gently above a brook splashing among rocks toward the Belle Fille River, on the windward slope of the island.

FRED WARD, BLACK STAR

people directly employed and another 100 indirectly employed. Perhaps most important, we are making new areas available for possible cultivation by building access roads. Some small farmers still pack bananas on their heads five miles over mountain trails to reach a roadside pickup station."

Except for parts of the Layou Valley, where Dom-Can operations began, the forests remained as before. Waterfalls tumbled into wet green glades; giant bamboo and towering trees festooned with orchids arched above; and, tying all together, lianas strangled their hosts. I found tilled areas hard to distinguish from forest, but occasional bunches of bananas or clusters of limes appeared through leafy frames.

I seemed engulfed in the sea of another planet, amid a confusion of hills and valleys as patternless as tide-ripped storm waves. As geographer John Macpherson wrote in *Caribbean Lands,* published in 1963, the island "is such a mass of peaks, ridges and ravines that in proportion to area it is more rugged than Switzerland."

Much of Dominica's character stems from the unusual rainfall. I soon encountered again the phenomenon Dominicans call liquid sunshine, a mist so fine it can be seen only when backlighted by the sun. Gently drifting from a cloudless sky, it gives a sensation more of coolness than of wetness. This is in addition to normal precipitation occurring in almost direct relation to the elevation.

"In sea-level Roseau we have an average rainfall of 75 to 80 inches a year," Gus Smith, one of the longtime residents, reaffirmed. "The Imperial Valley above the town gets about 130 inches. As you move higher it increases—to more than 200 inches near Pont Cassé, to 360 inches at Fresh Water Lake, and only the Lord knows what on the highest slopes of Morne Diablotin, which rises to 4,747 feet."

It was perhaps inevitable that Dominica saw the last stand of the Carib Indians.

Imperial Road threads a rain-soaked crease in the island's hilly spine. The highway links the capital city of Roseau on the leeward coast with the airport at Melville Hall on the Atlantic side. *Leptodactylus fallax* (right) weighs 2 pounds, almost twice as much as a North American bullfrog. Islanders cook the creature they know as *crapaud* and serve it as "mountain chicken."

The rugged terrain and dense forests were suited to their style of guerrilla warfare, and trails known only to them made pursuit virtually impossible.

The making of a Carib warrior began at birth. "As soon as a male child was brought into the world," wrote Jamaican Bryan Edwards in his history of the West Indies, published in 1793, "he was sprinkled with some drops of his father's blood.... The Father... believing that the same degree of courage which he had himself displayed was by these means transmitted to his son.

"One method of making their boys skillful even in infancy, in the exercise of the bow, was to suspend their food on the branch of a tree, compelling the hardy urchins to pierce it with their arrows, before they could obtain permission to eat."

Although not quite so tall as most Europeans of the era, the Caribs were a strong and muscular people. They painted their faces and bodies crimson and disfigured their cheeks "with deep incisions and hideous scars, which they stained with black, and they painted white and black circles round their eyes," continued Edwards.

Yet there was another side to these savage people. Although the Caribs considered all strangers enemies, they were, as Edwards recorded, "among themselves... peaceable, and towards each other faithful, friendly and affectionate."

A priest-historian who sailed through the islands at the end of the 17th century, Jean Baptiste Labat, declared in a work quoted by Edwards: "There is not a nation on earth more jealous of their independence than the Charaibes. They are impatient under the least infringement of it; and when, at anytime, they are witnesses to the respect and deference which the natives of Europe observe towards their superiors, they despise us as abject slaves; wondering how any man can be so base as to crouch before his equal."

As on other islands, the Caribs fought the invading Europeans. The earliest attempts to settle were successfully repulsed, and the Treaty of Aix-la-Chapelle in 1748 reaffirmed that Dominica belonged to the Caribs. But soon the familiar pattern began again: First came colonists drawn by land free for the taking, then soldiers to protect their interests.

Gunpowder and bullets overcame arrows and clubs, as elsewhere, but it took longer on Dominica. In fact, it was not until this century that the British succeeded in pinning the surviving Indians against a wild stretch of windward coast. Established in 1903, the Carib reservation consists of 3,700 acres extending in an eight-mile strip along the Atlantic.

Fighting flared even as late as 1930. After being charged with smuggling rum and tobacco, the Indians armed themselves with sticks and threw rocks at the police, who had fired on them, killing two Caribs and wounding others. Police reinforcements arrived but were driven off. It took a detachment of marines and star shells fired over the reservation by the cruiser H.M.S. *Delhi* to put down the rebellion.

Turning off the hard-surface highway to visit the Caribs, I wondered what I would find. In 1965 I had seen unhappiness and discontent among the Indians, stemming principally from the status of the reservation. Even before Dominica became an Associated State, questions had been raised in the legislature about the legality of the reserve's establishment. Searches of records reveal treaties with past chieftains, but no clearly defined grant of land in perpetuity by the Crown.

This time my four-wheel-drive Austin Champ—driven by Dennis Barnett, son-in-law of Alford Benoit, who had taken me in four years before—did not have to ford a river to reach Indian territory, nor did it have to climb a rutted mountain trail which became an impassable sluiceway after rains.

Fishing boat takes shape under artful hands. An adz-hollowed gommier trunk forms the shell of the dugout; upper planking adds freeboard. Dominicans fell the trees at the time of the new moon—to keep out grubs, they say. Similar to boats fashioned on St. Lucia and Martinique, the craft recalls the *kanaua* that once bore Carib warriors. Below, oarsman and paddler abet a hint of wind on their flour-sack mainsail, sprit-rigged for a twilight fishing run.

A bridge and a new road had been provided by the government.

Soon we passed Entwistle Rock, looming above the trees like a watchtower. I remembered the story told by Father Martin, former priest of the reservation's church, showing how the Caribs cling to their ancient legends: "I went to Entwistle Rock with the chief to look for a grotto where the old Caribs practiced their own religion.

"Our guide claimed his father had shown him the opening to the cave, but he couldn't find it; perhaps it had been blocked by a rockslide. In any case, the Caribs believe nobody could go in because it is guarded by a huge snake called *tête-chien*, meaning 'dog's head' in patois. The snake would eat any intruder. The legend also says the grotto connects with the sea, because during storms many *touloulou*, a type of sea crab, are found on the slopes of the Rock."

Beyond Entwistle Rock, we passed two children at the roadside. The little girl had long hair, straight and shiny black, high

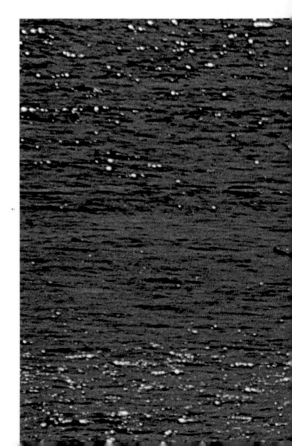

94

cheekbones, slanted almond eyes, and coppery skin. The boy looked the same except for a brush of short-cropped hair. Both could have been moppets in Hong Kong watching the workmen build *Sans Terre.*

Finally we arrived at the church maintained by the French order of the Sons of Mary Immaculate. Exposed in a small clearing overlooking the Atlantic, it has twice been blown down by hurricanes, but each time devotedly rebuilt by the Indians.

After looking at a small adjoining hall being constructed by volunteer workers— "We give one day of work a week because Father says we don't put enough in the collection box," I was told with a smile—I walked to the rectory to meet Father Paré, Father Martin's successor.

"The hall will give us something the Caribs here have never had," he explained, "a place for recreation. It will provide a place to gather, perhaps to listen to music, or even eventually to see a movie. Also I hope to display Carib basketry to sell. Almost 150 visitors came to the reservation last year because of the new road, and we are getting more all the time."

Like his predecessor, Father Paré is a wiry, dedicated man, with a sympathy and understanding that communicates itself to the simplest of his charges. "Things are better economically than before," he told me. "Trucks now haul out bananas, coconuts, and other produce. But problems remain. Perhaps you would like to discuss them with the chief."

Thirty-six-year-old Germandois Francis had recently been re-elected chief for a fourth three-year tenure. He welcomed me again at his house, a two-room structure of hand-hewn breadfruit planks perched on stilts in the center of a clearing worn smooth by shuffling feet. Like other Carib houses I had seen, it was small and bare, decorated only with pictures cut from magazines. Cooking was done outside, over a charcoal brazier or an open fire. A dog sniffed blackened kettles as we talked.

"The Royal Grant in 1903 was 3,700 acres of land, called the Carib Reserve; it belongs to the Carib people," the chief declared forcefully. "We hold the land in common, but the government wants to send in surveyors and divide our land into lots. This we oppose."

Chief Francis told me that there were 1,165 people in the reserve at the beginning of 1969, of whom about 600 were "pure" Caribs. When I first visited the reservation, in 1965, I expected to find "Black

Caribs," descendants of Indians and run-away African slaves. I had not been prepared for the Asian characteristics exhibited by many of the people I met.

I remembered another conversation with Father Martin, when I asked how many pure Caribs remained on the island. " 'Pure?' " he had repeated. "It depends on what you mean by the word. Few genealogical records exist, of course, but if you go on appearance—Mongolian features, straight black hair, slanted eyes, yellowish skin—about 400 Caribs survive. Their racial characteristics are extraordinarily strong."

From other sources I heard estimates of "pure" Caribs running down to zero, by those who scoffed at the notion that any had escaped intermingling of blood with other peoples through the centuries. Yet there is no denying the Caribs of Dominica form an ethnic group, descendants of a people who once held all the islands between Trinidad and Puerto Rico, and that

Descendants of conquerors: Only a few hundred "pure" Caribs remain of the thousands of man-eating Indians who burst from Brazilian jungles centuries ago to sweep the Lesser Antilles. Today they live on a reservation that stood as their forebears' last stronghold on Dominica. Chatting with the author, Chief Germandois Francis holds a crown-capped mace. Above, a Carib scrubs clothes in a creek. Features of old (below) and young alike show Asian ancestry.

96

they have come to a crossroads. Loss of their commonly held reserve could mean loss of tribal identity itself. It would be a final bitter blow for this remnant of a once mighty people.

Inaccessibility is an old story for Dominica. French islands on either side separate it from other British possessions; it lacks a protected harbor; and its jumbled terrain makes difficult the building of roads or expansion of the airport sandwiched between mountain and sea. Thus it has lagged behind its neighbors, but now there is solid progress in catching up.

It was not until 1956 that Roseau and Portsmouth, the two main towns, were linked. Although both face the Caribbean, the road snaked along the flatter Atlantic coast, resulting in a driving distance of more than 50 miles against 20 as a canoe might travel. Now a direct route on the Caribbean coast has been completed. Not far from the midpoint village of St. Joseph

I looked down on three land developments, called Emerald Hillside Estate, Castaways, and Maconcherie. Amid patterns of new streets, building lots awaited buyers.

Stages of island progress can be traced through the Fort Young Hotel in Roseau. Originally a British fortress, it became a police barracks, then in 1964 was transformed into a hotel, locally financed and managed. With the Silcotts, who were staying at the Fort Young after making the passage from Martinique aboard *Sans Terre,* I relaxed beside a swimming pool built in the center of the old parade ground. Above, rooms rimming the parapet looked over the sea. The Fort Young Company is planning not only expansion, but also the construction of another hotel —and a golf course, hard to imagine on the Dominica that was.

Another tourist need is being fulfilled by Dominica Safaris, organized in 1968 by Britisher Eric Lamb. "Of all the islands in

Windswept but serene, the Caribs' Catholic church stands above a desolate stretch of Atlantic coast. It holds a unique altar: an inverted fishing boat polished to gleaming brightness.

the Caribbean," he told me, "I found that Dominica offered the most unusual scenery. It was very difficult to get around, however, so we decided to make it easier for visitors to leave the beaten path. Our jeeps take them into the forests and to the more remote plantations, giving them a chance to swim in freshwater pools and rivers, and to shower under a waterfall. The drivers go through some of the world's most rugged country, but they always serve a gourmet lunch on a white tablecloth in some forest glade or on a beach. They have even been taught to pour wine correctly."

For me, no trip to Dominica would be complete without a visit to Springfield Plantation, high up the Imperial Valley, where I had stayed with owner John Archbold in 1947. Now a guesthouse as well as a plantation, Springfield is presided over by Millie Toussaint, John's housekeeper, who serves one of the finest native meals in all the West Indies.

This time Millie brought *écrevisses*—small freshwater crayfish—followed by a steaming platter of what looked like fried chicken. I knew from experience, however, that this was a delicacy that had never borne a feather. In the mountains of Dominica dwells a creature islanders call *crapaud* in its wild state, but "mountain chicken" when it appears on a plate.

Because of the heavy rainfall and deeply scored valleys, Dominica has many rivers; residents say there are 365, "one for every day of the year." Along the banks hunters capture the crapaud by night, when its eyes reflect torchlight. As we ate, I was again struck by the resemblance in texture and taste of mountain chicken to its plumed namesake. When the platter was empty Millie went through the ritual of showing us what we had enjoyed—a large frog with bulging eyes. As before, she laughed when she said, "If I show them to folks first, they won't eat any."

My appreciation of Dominica does not extend to the anchorage off Roseau, a roadstead open to every vagrant swell. Thus we passed our final night in Prince Rupert Bay, an excellent anchorage off Portsmouth. With daylight we awakened to the sounds of crowing roosters, braying donkeys, lowing cattle—and small boys looking for work, any work, from scrubbing the dinghy to fetching fruit and vegetables from the market. I could understand why local leaders show great concern over the need to provide jobs.

Ashore, we walked past tiny stores and weathered clapboard houses, plus a few buildings of concrete in pastel tints. Portsmouth is a town where dogs sleep in the center of the street, and sauntering pedestrians ignore the sidewalks. Somehow it reminded me of a remote Mexican coastal town, drowsing in the sun, waiting for a *mañana* beyond tomorrow.

After *Sans Terre* was clear of the land, I looked astern. "The highest mountains are usually obscured by clouds," the *Sailing Directions* note, but suddenly a caprice of the wind rent the misty veil. Like a moving spotlight the sun shafted across ridges and valleys, and then for a few minutes the whole mighty shape was visible, twisted into fantastic forms by the violent convulsions of nature. The forests, so dense their tree trunks had never known sunlight, accented rather than softened the effect.

Thus my final impression of Dominica was the same as on previous visits: It is the loneliest and most savagely beautiful of the Caribbee Isles. But, for the first time, I wondered how long it would remain so.

FRED WARD, BLACK STAR

Great pluming thickets wreathe bluffs along the windward coast of Dominica. Ceaseless pummeling by wind and ocean spray shaped the tangle of shrubs. The parrot *Amazona arausiaca* (left) perches in a lofty mountain haunt.

VII *Guadeloupe:*
Where Admirals Fought

In a shadow-dappled sea, the Îles des Saintes guard the southern approaches to Guadeloupe. The

O F ALL THE CHANNELS running among the island stepping-stones, none has witnessed greater drama than the passage between Guadeloupe and Dominica.

As Columbus sailed through on Sunday, November 3, 1493, on his second voyage, he bestowed names showing what was in his mind and heart: *Sancta Dominica,* because of its discovery on the Sabbath; *Sancta María la Gallante,* in honor of his flagship; *Todos los Santos,* for All Saints' Day, recently observed; and *Santa María de Gadalupe,* in gratitude to the Virgin to whom he had prayed for the success of his voyage. As we cruised toward Guadeloupe the same islands lifted above the horizon, bearing newer versions of the same names.

Perhaps divine guidance did bring Columbus to this particular landfall, because as more came to be known about the winds, currents, and geography of the New World, the Dominica Passage became one of the main arteries of access. For some four centuries, as long as commerce depended on sail, ships leaving Europe steered southward until they picked up the trade winds before turning westward, and the largest percentage of them entered the Caribbean by this same gateway.

Here, in April of 1782, Admiral Rodney caught up with the French fleet. We had been retracing his pursuit since leaving Gros Islet Bay on St. Lucia. The Battle of the Saintes is often cited as the turning point in West Indian history. French Admiral Comte de Grasse had tried to avoid

anquil waters once swarmed with European warships contending for control of the Caribbean.

A trick of the wind and bold tactics gave victory to Admiral Sir George Rodney (above) in the decisive Battle of the Saintes in 1782. As British and French fleets exchanged broadsides, shifting wind disorganized the line of French ships, commanded by Admiral Comte de Grasse (below). Rodney's ships drove through the gaps to cannonade the enemy from both sides. The crippled French fleet forfeited its admiral and his huge 110-gun flagship *Ville de Paris* (right) to H.M.S. *Barfleur*. Rodney's triumph firmly established British power in the Caribbean.

Guadeloupe's "split personality" offers volcanic heights on the west and coral-based lowlands on the east. Bisected by a channel, this department of France is home to 313,000 people.

conflict after leaving Martinique because he was under orders to rendezvous with the Spanish squadron waiting just off the north coast of Hispaniola, thus assuring a substantial military advantage for Britain's enemies. But when one of his ships was damaged in a collision, and in danger of capture, De Grasse turned back to assist and lost the chance to elude the British fleet.

The breeze was light and the sea calm as the two fleets sailed in parallel lines but in opposite directions. When the wind shifted, causing a gap in the column of French ships, Rodney seized his chance and cut through the enemy line. Five British ships followed and a sixth broke through at another point. The French fleet, divided and confused by the maneuver, came under fire from both sides.

The French fought bravely but hopelessly. When De Grasse finally struck his colors, some 400 of the 1,300 men on his flagship *Ville de Paris* were dead. The victory precluded any serious challenge to British sea power in the Caribbean, but Guadeloupe would change hands several times before being finally restored to France in 1815.

On this storied stretch of blue water, the Îles des Saintes lie like scattered chips of green mosaic. I had first known them as remote and rarely visited, peopled for the most part by a few fishing families; now I found them suburbs of Guadeloupe. Going ashore at Bourg des Saintes, on Terre de Haut, I was reminded that it is at once a privilege and a pain to have known a place as it was, then go back long after to see what it has become.

Eula and Alvin Daniels, seeing the village for the first time, found it charming, from the green painted statue on the quay symbolizing La Belle France to the cross on the hill above. But I remembered the quaint streets before they were lined with stucco villas, and the cross without its outline of garish electric light bulbs. Even more of a jolt was the slash through the hillside providing an approach to an airstrip which ran almost alongside a little cemetery with graves bordered by conch shells.

Yet whatever I had found in the way of change and progress before reaching Guadeloupe was by way of preparation. *"C'est la ville champignon,* 'the mushroom city,'" exclaimed Guy de Beaupré when he came aboard *Sans Terre* after we had moored

FRED WARD, BLACK STAR

Carnival madness erupts on Guadeloupe in early January, reaching a frenzy at Shrovetide. Calypso-singing revelers frolic in the streets through Ash Wednesday, when they reluctantly end their lively masquerade by "burying" Carnival. Then the quiet Lenten period begins.

off the yacht club in Pointe-à-Pitre. Guy, a Parisian, had emigrated to the French tropics and become a prosperous wine importer. He struggled for a moment to find a strong enough comparison, and burst forth: "*C'est un petit Chicago!* One week nothing, then *pouf!* the next, a new building!"

As dynamic Chicago had impressed Guy on a visit to the United States, so Pointe-à-Pitre struck me. On a fill across the harbor, towering structures mirrored the sunshine. Ships awaited their turn to come alongside the piers. New apartment buildings soared into the sky, some 16 stories high. Automobile traffic flowed in an endless torrent past Place de la Victoire, urged to greater speed by gesticulating gendarmes.

Leaving my deck for a closer look, I was even more impressed. The fill across Pointe-à-Pitre's busy harbor magnified into Pointe Jarry, a huge industrial complex. Four years before, dredges had just begun work; now a broad highway led past a new power plant, oil storage tanks, a cement factory, and a flour mill. Work had started on an oil refinery and on a mill to make wallboard from the pulp remaining from sugarcane after the juice is extracted.

Guadeloupe is a sugar isle. Facilities had been built on Pointe Jarry to handle an output of cane which in 1969 totaled 1,767,602 tons despite a drought during the growing season. Processing of the cane left 142,624 tons of sugar and 33,889 tons of molasses to be stored and shipped.

As I gaped at a gleaming aluminum warehouse almost as long as two football fields, I was told by plant watchman Jean Lagaril that the building was 590 feet long, 148 feet wide, and 82 feet high. "Trucks drive over scales, dump the sugar, and drive away, almost without stopping," he said. "If a ship is loading, the sugar doesn't stop. The 'flying carpet,' a conveyer belt, carries it along the overhead ramp to the dock. Below, there is a pipeline for molasses. Now we can load a 10,000-ton ship in two days, where it used to take at least ten."

Returning to Pointe-à-Pitre, I drove through Cité Bergevin et Malraux, a suburb which had not existed when I visited in 1965. Apartment houses marched in long ranks, bordering open playing areas. Detached from a school built of concrete and glass was a canteen, where students received free lunches. Across the highway a stadium was going up. Nearby, the post office stood like a giant honeycomb on stilts, the ground floor open for trucks.

Guadeloupe's modern buildings are saved from monotony by the ingenuity of the architects in keeping out tropic sun and rain, while admitting the breeze. In some the windows are deeply recessed behind horizontal cantilevered projections that resemble oversize Venetian blinds. Other buildings feature vertical fins, still others a beehive look. Most have overhanging outside balconies. Doors are painted every color of the rainbow.

So staggered was I by the new construction that I sought out the Sous-Préfet de Pointe-à-Pitre, Jean M. Petit, who administers one of Guadeloupe's three districts. "Between the beginning of 1965 and the end of 1968, La Société Immobilière, our state housing agency, built 2,811 *logements*, or apartments, each consisting of a kitchen, living-dining room, bath, from one to four bedrooms, and frequently a balcony," he told me. "This was financed almost entirely by the government. The goal of our 'Plan V,' which covers the years 1966 through 1970, is 12,000 logements, with an average occupancy of four inhabitants."

Yet Guadeloupe's population increase makes it difficult to keep pace. "In our population of 313,000," M. Petit continued, "there are 100,000 schoolchildren." The community of Lauricisque, called *Cité Transit* because it was intended as a temporary housing project where people would remain only until new apartments were ready for them, was bigger than before.

Driving through, I found that Cité Transit had taken on an air of permanency. Schools, churches, cafes, and stores had appeared among the small frame houses once scheduled for destruction. "Part of the reason is that many people don't want to go into the new apartments," explained my chauffeur. "Besides, there still aren't enough for those who do want to move."

Despite social progress, there is unrest. The Communist Party is strong, but split into pro-Moscow and pro-Peking groups. The Mao faction comprises the younger militants. Locally they are blamed for the riots of 1966, which left eight dead. The Moscow-oriented party controls more votes. Of Guadeloupe's 36 elected mayors six are Communist, including Dr. Henri Bangou in Pointe-à-Pitre, a heart specialist —"a very good, a very correct man," in the words of one of my acquaintances, "all types voted for him."

Pointe-à-Pitre may have taken its name from a Dutch sailor, "Pieters," who landed in 1654. Like other islands, Guadeloupe was a pawn of European politics, as I was reminded each time I looked toward Place de la Victoire. In 1794, during the French Revolution, the Reign of Terror reached out even to this tranquil outpost. A guillotine was erected in the park near where I now watched one of a series of night basketball games. Before the end of the paroxysm of hate that flowed from distant Europe, 1,200 Royalists were executed.

NATIONAL GEOGRAPHIC PHOTOGRAPHER WALTER MEAYERS EDWARDS

Human hoist lifts wrapped bananas into a vessel at Basse Terre, administrative capital of Guadeloupe. Inter-island ships (right) take on cargo at Pointe-à-Pitre. Nearby, in a community called "*Cité Transit*," former slum dwellers adjust to life in modern homes while urban planners work to rebuild their old neighborhoods.

NATIONAL GEOGRAPHIC PHOTOGRAPHER WINFIELD PARKS

Exploring from my central base, I found the wide, well-graded highways, *les routes nationales,* almost as impressive as the urban housing developments. Few rural areas are not completely accessible. Roadsigns are identical to those of France, and there are no speed limits on the open road.

Driving eastward from Pointe-à-Pitre as a guest of Maurice Devaux, a managing director of Crédit Guadeloupéen and the British vice-consul, I looked out on flat land, a reminder to me that Guadeloupe is not one island but two, with the Rivière Salée dividing the parts. The whole looks like a lopsided butterfly. Grande Terre, the eastern wing, dips into the Atlantic; the mountainous western wing faces the Caribbean and is named Basse Terre, which to early French voyagers who anchored in the lee of the island meant "sheltered land," rather than "low land." The two land areas are as different as the bodies of water bordering them.

Grande Terre is the sugarbowl. Behind fringing shallows patterned by reefs and beaches, the limestone interior is covered by fields of cane. The greatest elevation, 443 feet, occurs above the coastal town of Sainte Anne. This is in startling contrast to Basse Terre's volcanic peak of Soufrière,

whose 4,813-foot elevation makes it one of the highest mountains in the West Indies. Geographically, Guadeloupe combines many of the characteristics of the rugged Windward Islands, lying astern, with those of the flatter Leewards, such as Antigua and Anguilla, still ahead.

Our afternoon goal was Pointe des Châteaux, at the eastern tip of Grande Terre, which cleaves Atlantic swells like a ship's bow. Before reaching it, the wide highway had narrowed to a ribbon. A high-wheel cart loaded with sugarcane and drawn by oxen forced us to crawl along behind until we could find room to pass, the only interruption to the pace of modern progress I encountered on Guadeloupe.

"Here it is always rough," Mme Devaux exclaimed as we came to the base of the tortured peninsula. Seas which had gathered size and momentum for 3,000 miles dashed against rocks at our feet, filling the air with spray which blew like horizontal rain. Pointe des Châteaux—whose name might imply a cape dotted by mansions, seemed to hold nothing man-made except a cross interrupting the wild natural beauty. It held for me the fascination a sailor must always feel when confronted by the power of the ocean. Above the cresting surf lifted

Bounty from land and sea overflows in the market of Pointe-à-Pitre, Guadeloupe's economic center. Vendors entreat customers in patois or French—or, as at right, let the wares speak for themselves: in English, a red hind (spotted fish at top), barjacks (silvery gray), a rock beauty (orange and black), three goatfish (white), and a parrotfish (reddish, lower left).

NATIONAL GEOGRAPHIC PHOTOGRAPHERS WINFIELD PARKS (ABOVE) AND WALTER MEAYERS EDWARDS

the small flat-topped island of La Désirade. I could almost visualize the caravels of Columbus scudding by after the Admiral's second landfall in the New World.

A few days later, when I drove around Basse Terre in a rented Renault, I found it totally changed. The Caribbean lay placid in the wind shadow of a towering coast. On the slopes bananas grew in abundance, and on one of the scalloped beaches near Fort Royal I came across a bumper crop of the new staple, people intent on having fun.

"Except for Tahiti, this is the first Club Méditerranée outside the Mediterranean region," I was told by M. Michel Gallet, *Chef du Village*. "Please make yourself welcome among the *gentils membres*."

Informality is the keynote of this French tourist organization, which opened its first *village* on the Spanish island of Majorca in 1950, and now has 60 of them. On descending to the beach, I found myself freed of two of the basic problems of civilization: what to wear, and money. Swim trunks and a string of beads sufficed.

Edging my way through bronzed bodies to a poolside bar, I asked for a *pastis*, the anis-flavored apéritif popular in the south of France. To pay, I used part of my necklace. Beads marked with the club emblem of a trident superimposed on an "M" are the sole legal tender. Colors denote value. These are bought at the club office in advance. There are no pockets in a bikini!

"We are booked for the entire season ahead," I was told by M. Gallet after a sumptuous buffet lunch. "Only club members are admitted. Here 90 percent come from America, but we reserve 10 percent of our rooms for those who arrive from Paris. We opened in December 1968. Another village, on Martinique, will be ready this coming Christmas."

Continuing toward Guadeloupe's capital, also named Basse Terre, I was struck by the varied beauty of Guadeloupe's leeward coast. The Corniche d'Or is the sunset road, taking its name from the golden light cast by the sun as it drops toward the rim of the Caribbean. The way led through uplands covered with banana plants and swooped down to rim palm-fringed beaches. Flaming flamboyant trees in full bloom bordered the road.

Suddenly I found the way blocked by

"Un petit Chicago! — A little Chicago!" Thus a transplanted Parisian sums up fast-changing Pointe-à-Pitre, with 30,000 people the largest city of an island still mainly agricultural. Around the busy — and recently improved — harbor rise new industrial plants, new storage and ship-loading facilities for sugar and molasses, and new office buildings.

Cosmopolitan Christmas aboard *Sans Terre:* The author entertains friends with turkey American style, French champagne, a Mexican piñata overhead, and Santa figurines. Garlands frame a picture of his former yacht *Finisterre*.

massed humanity as I passed under a banner emblazoned *"Vive La France,"* on the outskirts of the town of Vieux-Habitants. Flags and tricolor rosettes decorated every house, and music blared from temporary cafes formed by intertwined green palm fronds. One bore a sign which translated: "Here you will eat well and can dance all day until you are tired." On a small stage, a juggler tossed balls into the air.

Parking my car, I made my way to a stage where a beauty contest was in progress. Lovely dark damsels paraded in bright print dresses. I quickly discovered that mini-skirts were popular—as *les mini-jupes.* In reply to my question, the man standing next to me explained, *"C'est notre fête locale,* our village fair. It is like a little carnival without costumes."

Yet in Guadeloupe it is impossible to go far without being reminded of the serious side of life. At the village of Bouillante,

JOHN LAUNOIS, BLACK STAR

which means "boiling," I had left the car to walk on a spongy field pocked by small holes filled with hot water. Near the sea what looked like an oil drilling rig was under construction, but I knew from my conversation with M. Petit that it represented an effort to measure volcanic heat and energy for possible industrial uses.

Although Pointe-à-Pitre is the commercial center of Guadeloupe, the administrative center is Basse Terre. A new section of elevated road ran along the waterfront there. I looked down on docks that were almost counterparts of Pointe Jarry, but designed for the loading of bananas, not sugar. Descending, I drove along wide avenues bordered by massive government buildings, long low blocks of gray concrete, impressive in size but disappointing after the multi-storied architecture of Pointe-à-Pitre.

Guadeloupe has as dependencies not only the nearby Saintes, La Désirade, Îles de la Petite Terre, and Marie Galante, but also more distant St. Barthélemy and the French half of St. Martin. Since 1946 Guadeloupe and the Saintes together have been an overseas department of France.

As time drew near for my departure toward those northern isles, I said goodbye to Eula and Alvin Daniels, who had to return to California. In *Finisterre* I had taken a short cut north, through the Rivière Salée, but this was no longer possible. The drawbridge permitting access to the channel was inoperative pending construction of a superhighway. So instead of ditch crawling, *Sans Terre* skirted the bold shores of Basse Terre.

From my flying bridge I followed the Corniche d'Or, seeing the island from a new perspective. The flamboyants were brush strokes of flame on variegated green. When Club Méditerranée came abeam, I found it hard to resist dropping anchor. Down below, I still had a few beads.

Long-boomed boats and coolie hats distinguish Saintes seamen. Introduced from the Orient, the hats are fashioned of bamboo and cotton.

Basse Terre's Soufrière (foreground) shares its name with other volcanoes scattered among the Caribbean isles. Dense, boggy moss hides the lava plug of the crater. On lower slopes grow liana-laced forests, and ferns with ten-foot leaves.

NATIONAL GEOGRAPHIC PHOTOGRAPHER WALTER MEAYERS EDWARDS

VIII Antigua: A Harbor's Storied Past

A key to British naval might in the Caribbean, English Harbour on Antigua provided a haven where warships refitted to avoid the long voyage across the Atlantic. A hilltop fort guards the entrance in this 19th-century aquatint.

ANTIGUA is the turning point in the island chain, the pivot, where the stepping-stones running northward from South America swing west toward Florida. In the days of sail Antigua commanded the entire Caribbean. Ships could swoop to the west with the trade winds astern, and vessels patrolling the bitterly contested southern islands could sail either north or south with the wind abeam.

Nature provided on Antigua one of the snuggest harbors in the West Indies, protected against hurricanes by a winding entrance channel and from invading enemies by surrounding heights. Here, at English Harbour, a great naval base and dockyard grew through the turbulent years. And, fittingly, here remains one of the most striking monuments to the golden age of sail.

When I entered in *Carib* in 1947, English Harbour was a tragic reminder of departed glory. The brickwork of the noble old buildings was crumbling, roofs had fallen in, and ironwork was rusting away. Later I learned that a report to the Colonial Office in London that same year described the condition of the dockyard as "deplorable." *Carib* had shared the anchorage with a single native sloop.

Now masts again surround the old stone quays. Ashore, the dockyard looks much as it must have when pigtailed seamen bent their backs at the capstans to careen their ships. I walked among buildings with evocative names: the Master Shipwright's House, Galley, Saw Pit, Copper and Lumber Store, Forge, Blacksmith's Shop, Paint Store and Cells, and the Cordage, Canvas and Clothing Store—goods and services essential to a "bundle of sticks held together by strings," as Jack Tar referred to his ship. I could almost feel myself among sailors of the past.

The miracle of restoration at English Harbour had begun when the Governor of the Leeward Islands, Sir Kenneth Blackburne, founded the Society of The Friends of English Harbour in 1951.

Winter visitors and devotees of sail on both sides of the Atlantic, including the British royal family, responded with contributions. Crews of visiting naval ships gave up their leaves to form work parties.

John Christian, who since 1962 has supervised maintenance and repair work, told me, "By searching Admiralty files in London, the original plans of these buildings were unearthed, just as they were drawn and approved by the architects and engineers. We were able to find carpenters right on Antigua who had retained the skills of the 18th-century shipwrights, familiar with the same tools. We came very close to duplicating the original work down to the last detail. Even the beams were hewn by hand with adzes, and pegged with wood instead of nailed."

As the abandoned base was reborn, it became a haven for a new generation of sailors, partly because of its discovery after the war by retired Comdr. Vernon E. B. Nicholson of the Royal Navy. In 1965 he told me the story.

"I sailed out from Ireland with my family in the schooner *Mollihawk* for a holiday," he said as we sat in his office, "but we were also looking for a nugget. Though we came into English Harbour before restoration work had begun, we felt we had found

At Nelson's Dockyard pleasure craft make fast to cannon barrels set in the quay where British frigates moored. Horatio Nelson, hero of Trafalgar, served at English Harbour as a captain from 1784 to 1787. High ground shields the landlocked harbor; Montserrat rises 30 miles away. Below, a youngster chins on a capstan; sailors of a bygone era labored at the drums, spooling in lines to careen ships. In Admiral's House, now a dockyard museum, the figurehead from H.M.S. *Atalanta* stands among other mementos.

NATIONAL GEOGRAPHIC PHOTOGRAPHERS JAMES L. STANFIELD (ABOVE) AND WINFIELD PARKS

something terrific. We offered *Mollihawk* for charter, and to our amazement, we were besieged. The next year we added a second vessel, a ketch. Later we began acting as brokers for other owners, some of whom were on their way round the world but wanted to make a few pounds."

Commander Nicholson even goes to the Mediterranean to recruit vessels; his fleet now numbers more than 60 yachts. The business launched by *Mollihawk* provided a fleet to match the progress of restoration and has had far-reaching effects on the economy and development of the islands.

The saga of the Nicholsons is part of the story of modern English Harbour. Rodney, one of the sons, met his wife when Irving Johnson's *Yankee* put in on the last leg of a globe-circling voyage. Desmond, the other son, also married an American girl, the daughter of a charterer. Now Commander and Mrs. Nicholson look down on a growing fleet of yachts and grandchildren from the terrace of an 18th-century powder magazine converted into a sailor's home ashore. Even the floors are caulked like a ship's deck, with scuppers so water can run off after a scrubbing.

Apart from English Harbour, the greatest visible change in the four years since

117

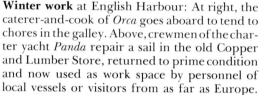

Winter work at English Harbour: At right, the caterer-and-cook of *Orca* goes aboard to tend to chores in the galley. Above, crewmen of the charter yacht *Panda* repair a sail in the old Copper and Lumber Store, returned to prime condition and now used as work space by personnel of local vessels or visitors from as far as Europe.

my 1965 visit also had to do with ships and the sea. Antigua bears so little resemblance to the islands already visited (except for Grande Terre on Guadeloupe) that it might be an ocean away. Despite a shoreline of scalloped bays, shallows extending far offshore made approach impossible for deep-draught cargo and passenger ships.

During the British colonial era, the port of St. John's was the seat of government for the Leeward Islands, and it remains the capital city and commercial center of Antigua now that the island has become an Associated State. But it was long a port in name only. Big ships had to lie as far as two miles offshore.

"Many tourists refused to come ashore when it was rough, so we lost some cruise-ship business. Also, our sugar and other cargo had to go out in lighters, taking long-

er to load and so increasing freight costs," I was told by Harbour Master George W. Benjamin. "A deepwater port has been a longtime dream of Antigua."

In December 1968 the goal was achieved. A channel 300 feet wide, 8,000 feet long, and 35 feet deep now leads to a pier of concrete and steel 1,300 feet long. "We can accommodate two cruise ships or four average cargo vessels alongside," Benjamin continued as we looked down on the dock from his office. "Sand pumped up by the dredges was used to fill in around Rat Island for the wharf area and a shopping plaza. The government intends to make Antigua a duty-free port for all tourist items."

Not far from the new port lies a marine fueling station, where the master of an ocean freighter can come alongside and say, "Fill her up." Duane MacFarland,

NATIONAL GEOGRAPHIC PHOTOGRAPHER JAMES L. STANFIELD

managing director of the West Indies Oil Company, Ltd., explained the operation: "Antigua is on a crossroads of world commerce. A ship taking coal from Hampton Roads to Rio or Japan, or grain from a Gulf of Mexico port to India, or iron ore from the east coast of South America to eastern Canada can carry more cargo and less fuel by making a stop here."

Antigua's refinery converts 15,000 barrels of Venezuelan crude oil daily into a wide range of products, from asphalt for building roads to jet fuel and premium gasoline. The products now are sold locally and to affiliates in Canada, but the company is expanding its Caribbean outlets.

The island is moving ahead on fronts other than maritime. "Transition to a dial telephone system is almost complete," I was told by Bradley T. Carrott, Minister of Public Works and Communications. "We are now conferring with engineers on the construction of a combination generating-desalinization plant. It not only will meet the future electrical needs of industry, but also will be capable of producing a million gallons of fresh water a day from the sea. We are also extending our runways to accommodate jumbo jets by May of 1970—next to Puerto Rico's we have the busiest airport in the eastern Caribbean, and we want to keep our lead."

Yet the most spectacular symbols of Antigua's link with the future are antennas silhouetted against the sky. Because of its position in relation to the launch pads at Cape Kennedy, the island has played an important role in the U. S. space program. On my 1965 visit I had toured the Air Force's Missile Tracking Station, a key

Swirling cattle egrets prey on snails and insects exposed by a slashing machete in a field of sugarcane

point in the Atlantic Missile Range. There I had seen a telemetry antenna used to pick up electronic noises from orbiting satellites. At its base donkeys grazed; the Antiguans had reserved pasture rights on the 600 acres leased to the U. S. Air Force.

Now with Carl Schumacher, a receiver-technician, I visited another tracking station, this one serving as a link in the Manned Space Flight Network to monitor the first 11 Apollo flights. Passing a NASA Group Achievement Award "for exceptional support . . . in tracking, maintaining communications, and acquiring data . . . [during] the first manned lunar orbit mission," we entered a room banked with computers, dials, and digital clocks counting down the final 24 hours to the launch of Apollo 10 toward lunar orbit.

Never had passing seconds seemed so linked with destiny. To help him probe a universe billions of years old, man had learned to fragment time into incredibly small units. As we walked, Carl commented casually, "This atomic clock is accurate to one second every 6,000 years." He continued speaking in terms my brain refused to absorb. Finally, after passing between banks of intricate apparatus, we came to a stainless-steel control desk. Set into the center of it was—of all things—an ordinary duckpin ball, the upper half exposed. Through a window we could see a dish-shaped tracking antenna on a tower well away from the control center. "When I move the ball, it will control the antenna," said Carl. "Watch!"

With his fingertips he spun the bowling ball, and the huge structure obediently changed azimuth and elevation to follow every movement, as it did when being

The island's chief crop grows on some 12,000 acres.

canoes. Third, a source of water. Fourth, a hummock to shelter them from the wind. And fifth, flat land for growing manioc, from which cassava cakes were made. When I found a site combining these features, I began to dig. This is what I found!"

Climbing down into a trench, I saw embedded shells, pottery fragments, fishbones, and even the rim of a pottery griddle used for baking. "Radiocarbon tests place the upper deposits at about A.D. 1100, but deeper layers go back another 700 years," Fred continued. "Until the Caribs got this far up the chain, not long before Columbus arrived, the Arawaks lived what must have been a rather idyllic life. In fact, you can say that what made a good site for a pre-Columbian tribal settlement is frequently good for a modern resort community."

Although Antigua's average rainfall is only 42 inches a year, the island was deluged during my stay in March 1969. In just ten minutes the rain gauge at the police station caught one inch. Cisterns were overflowing for the first time in years and fields of sugarcane glistened as roots thirstily absorbed the water.

Usually, the silver lining for the rare rain cloud on Antigua is almost perpetual sunshine, inviting escape to the tropics when skies turn gray at home. Antigua was one of the first islands to welcome escapees from winter when the post-World War II influx began. Beaches washed by water in pastel tints of green and blue surround the island, encouraging the building of hotels and guesthouses. "Tourists are supplanting sugarcane as our chief crop," a St. John's businessman had told me in 1965. Then, the island had 23 hotels and guesthouses; now there are 37, totaling some 900 rooms.

Each day, after outings around the island, I returned to English Harbour with a feeling of gratitude. Not only did the snug cabin of Sans Terre beckon, but also the quaint hostelry known as the Admiral's Inn, completed in 1788 as the Engineers' Offices. I dined under hand-hewn beams admirably in keeping with the restoration. My memories of the inn include watching a goat race from the terrace, when children from a nearby village brought their pets to compete for a prize. The goats—and a few sheep—were dressed in carnival splendor, even to lipstick and wristwatches. On Saturday nights, couples danced under the

aimed to lock on to and follow an object in space. When Carl tried to explain all that was involved, I recalled those grazing donkeys, feeling more kinship with them than with the men exploring space.

Fortunately, the other end of the Antigua time scale was easier to comprehend. Not even on Dominica had the existence of vanished peoples seemed so real. In 1965 I had visited excavations made by Fred Olsen, a retired chemical engineer and amateur archeologist. Close to the private resort at Mill Reef he had shown me the site of an Arawak settlement.

"Not long after moving to Antigua I asked myself what a tribe would want in an encampment," Fred explained, "and I decided there were five requirements. First, they would need an offshore reef for fishing. Second, a sand beach for pulling up

121

Inches from the floor, a limbo dancer contorts his body and wriggles under a flaming bar in an island night club. Dancing couples swing to the rhythm of a steel drum band at the Admiral's Inn. The building, finished in 1788, provided storerooms and offices for the English Harbour engineers.

Deep blue of the Caribbean invades the transparent waters of shallow Dickinson Bay. With little rainfall, Antigua counts sunshine and sand among its greatest assets. This mile-long curve of beach alone affords two hotels.

Sprinting for prizes, goats and sheep outrun owners. A gaudy costume fails to hinder the leader.

stars as the music of a steel band reverberated from fortified hillsides.

The most recent lure for sailors is Antigua Sailing Week, which takes place the first week of June. Yachts arriving from the south compete informally from Guadeloupe to English Harbour, and then begin a round of racing festivities. The days frequently end with new anchorages, and parties ranging from a beach barbecue by torchlight on uninhabited Great Bird Island to a ball at the Admiral's Inn when prizes are presented to winning yachtsmen by His Excellency the Governor. Under the circumstances, there are no losers.

THE EARLIEST REFERENCE to English Harbour appears in a letter of 1671, when the Governor of the Leeward Islands wrote the Council for Foreign Plantations in London that it was "so land locked as to be out of danger of hurricanes." In 1704 Berkeley Fort was built on a finger of land at the entrance, and three years later the 44-gun *Adventure* became the first Royal Navy ship to careen, heaving herself down with the weight of her own cannon, much as local fishing boats still careen with ballast and tackles.

It was at the end of the 18th century that English Harbour reached its zenith. By then the dockyard could service almost any need of the men-of-war warping through the entrance in a constant stream. Enormous cisterns provided water, and fortifications ranged from a chain stretched across the entrance each night in time of war to gun emplacements on Shirley Heights that commanded every approach. More than a thousand troops, including artillerymen, formed the shore guard. Even a member of the royal family lived there, H.R.H. Prince William Henry, Duke of Clarence, who became William IV, the "Sailor King."

Despite English Harbour's martial history, only once was a shot fired in anger there, and only once was an attack attempted. In 1798 two young officers got into a heated argument over who had the duty of rowing guard in the harbor that night, when both wanted to go to a ball. Each claimed seniority, and ordered the other to remain on the station. Finally Lt. Thomas Pitt, the second Baron Camelford, demanded to know if Lt. Charles Peterson still refused to obey his orders. Upon the reply, "I do!" Lord Camelford shot his rival dead. Tried and acquitted, the young peer later reached the end of his own turbulent career when he was killed in a duel.

The attempted attack took place in 1803 when the governor of French Guadeloupe dispatched 700 men in 13 schooners to carry out a surprise invasion. The force did not even get near enough for the shore batteries to go into action. A cruising frigate, H.M.S. *Emerald*, intercepted the fleet in the channel, captured three vessels, and sent the rest scurrying.

English Harbour in the 18th century was a crowded and lively place, an endless pageant. Horatio Nelson, then the young captain of H.M.S. *Boreas*, sailed from here to neighboring Nevis to woo and win a bride given in marriage by the Duke of Clarence. Admiral Rodney, after making himself master of the Dutch island of Statia in 1781, sent some of the captured material to Antigua, and a large brass flowerpot of Dutch origin now in Clarence House is probably part of the booty.

In such surroundings it is easy to recapture the past. As I walked past the Officers' Quarters I recalled an anecdote related by maintenance supervisor John Christian. "It is not surprising that people who can see ghosts see them here," he had said musingly. "I think I saw one myself for the first time in my life. Late one afternoon in my bedroom I put down a book and before me stood an officer dressed in the uniform of Nelson's day—dark blue cutaway coat, white stock, pigtail, and all. He was in profile, and I saw him put his hand to his face and cough nervously. The poor chap looked exactly like a man preoccupied with problems, about to have an unpleasant interview.

"Later I found from old drawings that the building called the Admiral's House did not exist when Nelson was stationed here between 1784 and 1787. His house was actually on the site of the present Officers' Quarters. So I'm convinced I saw a ghost who came to be ticked off by the boss!"

Sea-carved Devil's Bridge funnels spray from Atlantic rollers that surge against Antigua's northeast coast. Cautious visitors hold hands for safety on the rugged ledge. The low-lying island rises only 1,300 feet at its highest point.

IX   *Montserrat and Nevis:*
Mountains to the Clouds

Wearing a misty tiara, a volcanic peak rises on Nevis, once "Queen of the Caribbees." Freight lighte

W HEN *SANS TERRE* ROLLED her way downwind from Antigua, bound for Nevis, a new crew member sat beside me on the flying bridge. But perhaps "crew member" is not the proper term for Capt. Walter Leslie Mortimer Brown, D.S.O., O.B.E., D.S.C., even though he referred to himself as "*Sans Terre*'s deckhand."

After achieving a distinguished record in the Royal Navy during World War II, "Bruno" Brown retired from service in 1958 and sailed for the West Indies aboard his own little ship, *Dayspring,* a fishing trawler that had been converted into a yacht. Pleased with English Harbour, he stayed on there to become captain of the charter schooner *Freelance,* one of the largest vessels of the Nicholson fleet. So for nearly ten years he has daily observed Caribbean weather— and some of his findings run counter to popular belief.

"There are really no seasons here, as people think of them in northern latitudes," he explained. "The main difference between January and June is the length of the days. Statistically it no doubt can be proved there is more wind or rain, or it is hotter or colder, at one time of the year than another, but a visitor on a short vacation is not likely to notice any difference. A lot of the folklore is misleading. Twice I've crossed from Antigua to Guadeloupe on Christmas Day over a glassy calm sea without enough wind to fill the sails, and yet

ait on a sun-flecked sea beside a low-lying arm of St. Kitts. A narrow strait separates the two islands.

NATIONAL GEOGRAPHIC PHOTOGRAPHER WINFIELD PARKS

everybody talks about the Christmas winds. In summer—when it is supposed to be calm and hot—there are often spells like now: cool, and with plenty of wind."

As we talked, Montserrat was in sight on the port beam. Heavy seas had caused me to abandon my plan to visit it by boat. I knew from experience that the roadstead of Plymouth would be uncomfortable if not downright dangerous. So I had left *Sans Terre* snug in English Harbour earlier in the week to make the journey by plane, vaulting the 35 miles in 15 minutes.

On landing, I took a taxi to Plymouth, the capital, on the Caribbean coast, where once I had stayed a week at Government House as the guest of Charlesworth Ross, then Acting Administrator. The road climbed steeply over the central spine. On both sides stretched fields of Sea Island cotton, sweet potatoes, tomatoes, and banana plants and groves of lime and coconut trees—Montserrat, I recalled, is known as the "Garden Island of the West Indies."

In the Caribbean melting pot of races and nationalities Montserrat is the pinch of Irish. It is divided into parishes: St. Anthony, St. George's, and St. Peter. Somehow St. Patrick was slighted, but there is a St. Patrick's village on the southwest coast, near O'Garra's Estate and Galway's Soufrière, a reminder that the Irish settled on Montserrat in the 1630's. Later, during Cromwellian times, other Irish arrived, many as exiles. In some rural areas the brogue lingers as a reminder of the Ould Sod, coming as a surprise to a visitor asking directions of a dusky islander.

Arriving at Government House, I had a moment of nostalgia. All was as I remembered it: the sentry box at the gate, the small garden filled with tropical blooms, the rusted cannon pointing toward the harbor, the green mansion set off by white

N.G.S. PHOTOGRAPHER WINFIELD PARKS (BELOW) AND TED SPIEGEL, RAPHO GUILLUMETTE

An islander models for artist Eva Wilkin in a studio where iron rollers once crushed sugarcane. The converted mill, last of its kind to operate on Nevis, ceased production in 1940.

Time-ravaged ruin of Eden Brown Estate enshrines a legend: In the 18th century a rich planter built the great house and furnished it lavishly for his daughter; but it was abandoned, locked and sealed, when her bridegroom died after a drunken wedding-eve duel. From that day to this, no one has lived there.

railings, shutters, and columns, and the shamrock surmounting the central gable. Even the British ensign still flew from the flagstaff, signifying Montserrat's continuing colonial status.

Administrator Dennis Raleigh Gibbs welcomed me to the vine-covered veranda. When I explained why I had come by air rather than by sea, Mr. Gibbs exclaimed, "Ah! Our number-one economic project is to build a deepwater port!" He went on to explain that feasibility studies had been made for two jetties, allowing ships drawing up to 30 feet to dock at the ends, while smaller vessels and yachts could lie in the protected area between.

I found that Montserrat was not lagging behind its fellow CARIFTA members in economic progress. "During the '60's our gross national product increased by as much as 11.5 percent annually," said Mr. Gibbs. "That was due mostly to a 'resident tourist industry'—the building of homes by people who live in them all winter. Even in our peak season more people are living in their own or rented homes than in hotels. There are still only 80 or so hotel rooms, but in 1969 there were five developments with a total of 186 homes built mainly for Americans and Canadians."

Montserrat is a friendly island. People along the roadside waved and spoke as Bill White, an American settler, showed me the new sights. We passed an emerald-green golf course looking over the sea, then drove through a community of pleasant homes, where four years earlier bulldozers had been at work. Lifting my gaze to the towering slopes beyond, I was reminded of an anecdote Charlesworth Ross had related to describe the contours of Montserrat: "One day I met a woman with her arm in a sling. I asked her, 'Bridget, what happened?' and she answered, 'Yer honor, I wuz warkin' in

129

me field when I fell out and broke me arrm on the road, begorra!' "

From the deck of *Sans Terre*, as she rolled on westward toward Nevis, Montserrat looked like a vest-pocket Dominica, steep and verdant, with spring-fed streams rushing down the mountainsides. To assure my return, I had quaffed the waters of a stream called Runaway Ghaut. This, according to legend, means a traveler must someday come back. Tacked over my chart table as a further reminder was the burgee of the Montserrat Yacht Club—a green shamrock on a white background, begorra!

As Montserrat dropped astern, Nevis, now an Associated State, grew clearer ahead. I saw the symmetrical peak and a hovering cloud that looked like snow. As *Sans Terre* moved closer, the illusion of snow turned into a creampuff of cloud riding above checkerboard slopes of green and yellow fields. Conical stone towers, the bases of windmills once used in crushing sugarcane, dotted the landscape.

I think of Nevis, more than any other island, as symbolizing the sugar economy of the 18th and early 19th centuries—the era that passed with Britain's abolition of slavery in 1834. Just as Antigua's English Harbour represented the zenith of British sea power in the Caribbean before the introduction of steamships, so the sugar estates of Nevis gained acclaim for that island as "Queen of the Caribbees."

Instead of dropping anchor in the roadstead at Charlestown, I continued north to the protected cove off Tamarind, the retirement home of G. Edward Willis and his wife Peg. They had settled where a hook of land north of Pinney's Beach forms the island's best shelter from marching swells. I had not forgotten an invitation pending since my last visit.

The arrival of *Sans Terre* coincided with a gathering of neighbors, and with typical island hospitality my crew and I were included. Thinking of Nevis as somewhat off the beaten track, I was astonished to find myself speaking to a man who regularly commuted to work—in New York.

"My wife and I decided we had had enough of big-city life," I was told by Edwin H. Mullen, a Pan-American Airways pilot, "and we didn't care for the suburbs. So we moved to Nevis a couple of years ago. I work two weeks out of New York,

Supple cricketer whirls like a pinwheel as he bowls a fast ball during practice on Montserrat. Training on village fields such as this, players aspire to the West Indies test match teams, chosen annually to compete with the best in the world.

Small spectator maintains wide-eyed interest in track events without missing a bite of ice cream. A rooter at a Montserrat meet, he watched girls skip to the ribbon with jump ropes (right). Earlier contestants raced with soft-drink bottles balanced on their heads.

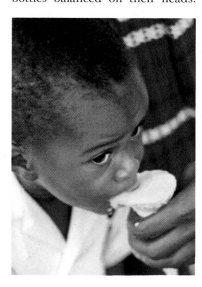

then have a few days off. I hop a plane and am here almost as fast as some of my friends can get home through the traffic."

The next morning we witnessed an episode dramatizing the other end of the transportation scale, a reminder that although jets whiz overhead, there is an unhurried pace to island life. At first light the sloop *Unity II* sailed in to anchor as close to the sand as her draught permitted. The crew sent lines ashore; animals that had waited tethered under the trees were driven into the water. A sling rigged from a halyard to the masthead lifted protesting beasts over the rail and lowered them into the hold. First came sheep, then goats, then an enormous sow, then three cows. Finally, when I thought there was no room for

anything more, a very buxom lady — a "first-class passenger," in Bruno's words — was ferried out to the miniature Noah's ark.

Only by driving the road that skirts much of Nevis's coastal plain can a visitor fully appreciate the extent of planting during the colonial period. Cane fields ring the island, stretching unbroken from the lower slopes of the volcanic central cone to the sea. Ruins of the estate mansions are stately and spacious even in neglect. Sadly, many were used as quarries, with beautifully cut and fitted stones hauled away for use in new buildings.

The last working sugar mill on Nevis was Clay Ghaut Estate. The word "ghaut" is often found on islands where indentured East Indian laborers were introduced when slaves were freed; it is said to be their word for ravine or small stream.

Clay Ghaut's present owner is Miss Eva Wilkin, one of the few surviving descendants of the colonial plantocracy. The word "plantocracy," a combination of "planter" and "aristocracy," no doubt aptly described estate owners during the golden years when sugar was king.

Told of my coming by dial telephone, a rare intrusion of modernity into the tranquillity of Nevis, Miss Wilkin awaited me at the door of a stone windmill tower she had converted into a studio. Since my visit in 1965 she had added a tiny kitchen and a bath and had transformed the upper floor into a bedroom. As we sat surrounded by her paintings, she showed me faded photographs of the same tower when it was a working mill.

"I came across these recently, and thought they would interest you," she said. "They were taken in the late 1930's, shortly before we stopped making sugar."

Dashing Capt. Horatio Nelson wooed a young Nevis widow while serving at English Harbour. A faded entry in the Fig Tree Church marriage register records the success of his courtship: "1787. March 11th. Horatio Nelson, Esquire, Captain of his Majesty's Ship, the Boreas, to Frances Herbert Nesbit, Widow." The mansion on Montpelier Estate, scene of the wedding, has vanished. So has the house nearby where, according to tradition, Alexander Hamilton was born. A plaque (left) commemorates the American statesman. It gives his birth date as 1757, two years later than that favored by many scholars.

wood—turned iron rollers that had been brought out long ago in a sailing ship. The cane was crushed by such rollers in this room; the juice ran through wooden troughs to an outside shed and into large kettles fired by dried bagasse.

"After the juice thickened, it was ladled into slatted wooden trays to cool. When the molasses dripped away it left muscovado—raw-sugar crystals—retaining much of the color and taste of molasses. Once, almost every estate on Nevis made sugar the same way. Today we buy it in paper bags at the grocery, like the rest of the world."

Part of the 210 acres remaining of Clay Ghaut borders on Fawcett Estate. "Alexander Hamilton's mother was born there," Miss Wilkin reminded me as we stood looking over the fields. "She was Rachael Fawcett, said to have been of French Huguenot extraction." Later in Charlestown, we saw

I saw huge sails of canvas fixed to lattice-work vanes and, on the opposite side of the tower, a long boom that reached to the ground. A mule hitched to the boom rotated the wooden upper part of the tower so the vanes would face the wind. Around the base of the tower workers unloaded sugarcane from carts and laden donkeys. Women and children sat among piles of bagasse, the remains of the crushed stalks, waiting for a taste of "skimmer," the natural sugar candy that formed on top of cane juice boiling in iron kettles.

Miss Wilkin continued:

"As wind spun the vanes above, gears with cogs of lignum vitae—a very hard

the site believed to be Alexander Hamilton's birthplace. There a plaque commemorates him as "one of the founding fathers of the United States of America."

During the period that the great houses flourished, the thermal springs of Nevis became the most fashionable cure outside Europe. The first known reference to them appears in an account by Captain John Smith, who dropped anchor here in 1607 on his way to Virginia. His company came ashore to fill water casks and replenish the wood for the galley fire.

In the course of their exploration several of the crew presumably touched the leaves or bark of manchineel trees, which blister and irritate like poison ivy. The sap is so potent that Caribs smeared it on arrow points to make them more deadly. Fortunately, John Smith's men later "found a great Poole, wherein bathing themselves, they found much ease . . . [and] were well cured in two or three dayes."

Later travelers reported similar relief for afflictions ranging from gout to leprosy, so in 1793 the Bath Hotel was built to receive visitors not only from neighboring islands but also from England—no mean compliment for the waters of Nevis when the round-trip voyage took weeks.

Resisting time, hurricanes, and earthquakes, the Bath Hotel is still impressive, and is scheduled to be open again to guests in 1971. As I noted stonework so perfectly fitted it needed no mortar, and walked under vaulted ceilings, I could see why the hotel was reputed to have cost £40,000, an enormous sum in slave-labor days.

This time I sampled the thermal baths, walking down wooden steps in semidarkness to five tile pools, larger and deeper than bathtubs, each screened off by wooden walls. When my eyes adjusted to the dim

light, I found a rusted hook for my clothes. Each bath maintains its own constant temperature, the mildest being 103° F. and the warmest 108°. While there I too "found much ease," stemming from a sensation of buoyancy and relaxation.

Charlestown bears out the theme of vanished glory. Nearly leveled by fire in 1873, the town was rebuilt partly in stone and partly in wood, but almost invariably the roofs are of corrugated steel. Donkeys share the streets with automobiles. Natural crooks cut from trees—the same that form the frames of local boats—support the upper verandas of many homes.

Overlooking a small triangular town "square," the Court House recalls black days in the career of Horatio Nelson. After he rigidly interpreted an act restricting trade with the infant republic of the United States and intercepted four ships off Nevis in 1785, irate merchants persuaded the American ship captains to file suit against him. The law had been largely ignored by government officials and even by other officers of the Royal Navy, so the Nevisians regarded Nelson's seizure of their property as virtually an act of piracy.

The President of the Nevis Council offered to stand Nelson's bail, and the Admiralty sustained the captain, but his popularity with the islanders reached a low ebb. Nevertheless, with the aplomb he was to show right down to his death in the cockpit of *Victory* at the Battle of Trafalgar, Nelson went about his business. Each day he paced the lookout on Saddle Hill with his spyglass, and even wooed a local lady.

In the register of Fig Tree Church, near Charlestown, I again bent to decipher an entry in faded ink on crumbling paper: "1787. March 11th. Horatio Nelson, Esquire, Captain of his Majesty's Ship, the Boreas, to Frances Herbert Nesbit, Widow." The marriage took place in the great house of Montpelier Estate, now vanished. The future King William IV of England, then the Duke of Clarence, sailed over from English Harbour to give the bride away.

With streamers of fireworks—and bright fabrics —Montserrat celebrates the first visit of its sovereign. The royal yacht *Britannia* (right) brought Queen Elizabeth II and Prince Philip into Plymouth harbor, where costumed islanders waited to perform in their honor on February 19, 1966.

X St. Kitts:
Sugar From the Fields

Trailing a boiling wake, a yawl reaches across The Narrows off St. Kitts. Early British and Fren

ST. KITTS AND NEVIS could be called sister islands, but, to be historically exact, mother and daughter would be better. For St. Christopher, better known by its nickname, was the site of the first permanent English colony in the Caribbean.

Captain Thomas Warner landed in 1624 with his wife and eldest son and about 13 settlers to challenge fate—which took the form of fierce Caribs, Spaniards jealously protecting their "lake," undergrowth to be cut before cultivation could begin, and tropical diseases. The colony prospered and sent out shoots to other islands, beginning with Nevis. St. Kitts is therefore the Mother Isle of the British West Indies.

As we crossed The Narrows, I was again reminded of other paired islands I had seen from the deck of a small cruiser: Tahiti and Moorea in the Pacific, Ischia and Capri in the Mediterranean, all different but all conveying the same sharp stab of beauty.

Normally, vessels ply directly between Charlestown on Nevis and Basseterre on St. Kitts, a distance of 13 miles, but rough seas dictated that we hug the coast and cross the channel at its narrowest point, where it is only two miles wide. Long swells from the open ocean grew steep and cresting as they came on soundings, and were further churned by currents running through the slot. Wind-driven spray stung us on the flying bridge, and I wondered whether it would be possible to anchor in the exposed roadstead at Basseterre.

ettlers on the island drove out the Carib Indians—and were in turn banished for a time by a Spanish fleet.

NATIONAL GEOGRAPHIC PHOTOGRAPHER WINFIELD PARKS

Under the lee of St. Kitts the sea smoothed, but off the town ahead I could see vessels rolling and plunging. Against my better judgment I maneuvered to a position near the dock, and Bruno let go the anchor. When we fetched up on the chain, normally docile *Sans Terre* reacted like a wild stallion feeling the halter.

"Do you think we can make it?" I shouted, pointing shoreward.

"We can try," Bruno replied calmly.

Somehow we launched the dinghy from the stern davits and got aboard, Bruno running the outboard while I crouched amidships, ready to leap for the pier. We never made it. Seas turned to surf as we neared the beach. Bruno skillfully avoided a series of breaking crests threatening to swamp us.

Getting back to *Sans Terre* was not easy, but finally we raised the anchor and returned to a cove we had looked into earlier. A point of land broke the swells, and a ruined pier remaining from the days when salt had been exported made it possible to

get ashore. In the afternoon we walked sparse scrubland that an abnormal downpour had turned into a quagmire. The next day I finally reached Basseterre, after hiring a boat capable of landing there.

Like St. Vincent, St. Kitts resembles a carefully tended garden, as indeed it is, except for the low southeastern peninsula, where rain rarely falls. Its Carib name is Liamuiga, the "Fertile Isle." For more than three centuries islanders have worked the fields. Cane grows in a broad belt around 4,134-foot Mount Misery and the lesser peaks forming the central spine. A narrow-gauge railway carries the crop to a factory. So dominant is sugar in the economy that it accounts for some 90 percent of export revenues. Other sugar islands, such as Antigua and Barbados, have had in recent years the cushion of tourist spending, but St. Kitts remains tied to its one crop. The estates experiment with others but always come back to their traditional planting.

Since becoming an Associated State on

NICHOLAS POCOCK, 1784, NATIONAL MARITIME MUSEUM, GREENWICH, ENGLAND

Sails shot full of holes, French ships vainly attack British men-of-war that block them from their siege base on St. Kitts. In the battle in 1782, Comte de Grasse found himself tricked out of position by Sir Samuel Hood, who feigned retreat to provoke pursuit, then sailed back to cut off his enemy. Tactically brilliant, Hood's feat failed to accomplish his goal of lifting the French siege of Brimstone Hill (map, below).

February 27, 1967, St. Kitts has had more political growing pains than its neighbors. The most publicized was the breaking away of Anguilla, which, with Nevis, had been grouped with St. Kitts in the colonial era. When statehood was granted, the triumvirate was preserved, and St. Kitts remained the seat of government, with Robert Bradshaw as Premier.

Nevis accepted its new status, but on May 30 Anguilla reacted by announcing its secession from the new federation and promptly forcing out a garrison of St. Kitts policemen. I had found sympathy for Anguilla's cause elsewhere during my cruise. "First the island was a colony of Britain, but administered from Basseterre," I was told more than once, "which made it the colony of a colony. Then, when independence was in sight, Anguilla found itself about to remain a colony of St. Kitts."

Months before the rebellion, the federation's Legislative Council voted to prohibit public meetings without a police permit.

PAINTING BY HEINRICH BERANN

Mount Misery
ST. CHRISTOPHER
(ST. KITTS)
N
Site of Le Château
de la Montagne
Caribbean Sea
Brimstone Hill
Fort
Frigate Bay
Basseterre
NEVIS
The Narrows
Caribbean Sea
Clay Ghaut
Estate
Pinney's Beach
Charlestown
Saddle Hill

When Anguilla broke away, Premier Bradshaw proclaimed a state of emergency throughout the federation. On June 10 the power station and police headquarters in Basseterre were attacked. The Premier ordered the arrest of those suspected in the shootings, some of whom were leaders of the People's Action Movement, the opposition party. I knew that much had occurred in the two years since Anguilla's secession, and I determined to discover for myself the current state of things on the island by visiting it if I could.

After buying a local newspaper, the *Democrat*, in Basseterre, I quickly saw that Anguilla was not the only problem plaguing St. Kitts. Under a banner headline, "Every Dollar Counts," I read that the sugar factory at Basseterre had been forced to curtail production for 196 hours to date, "almost entirely due to an inadequate delivery of cane from the estates." Each hour

"Gibraltar of the West Indies": The garrison of Brimstone Hill Fort gained glory even while losing the only battle it fought. In 1782 a British force of about 1,200 men withstood 6,000 attacking Frenchmen for nearly a month. The courage of the defenders so impressed the French that after the fort fell they let the king's troops go with flags flying. Visitors (below) stand on the ramparts. Statia rises in the distance.

of inactivity cost the mill—and the island economy—a loss of 125 tons of cane from the six-month grinding season, and "every dollar counts."

Here I was encountering a situation almost universal in the West Indies, one of the most serious problems confronting the leaders of the emerging states. It was summed up by George T. Warren, general manager of the sugar factory. "Once you educate people, they don't want to go back to the fields with a hoe, or a cane knife," he told me above the roar of machinery. "Yet despite the increase in tourism, and plans for industrial development, agriculture for the foreseeable future must remain the basis of island prosperity."

While I learned that cultivation of cane had dropped from 16,000 to 12,500 acres since my last visit, the decrease was not apparent. Rich fields bordered the road as I climbed inland by taxi toward the ruins of Château de la Montagne, once a stronghold of French colonial government.

Although the Kittitians are proud of being part of the oldest English settlement in the West Indies, the island equally deserves the title of "Mother of the French Antilles." Site of a French colony before either Martinique or Guadeloupe, it once managed the affairs of the larger daughters.

French settlement on St. Kitts began about a year after the English arrived. Thomas Warner had sailed back to England

Open roadstead of Basseterre throbs with the vending of pottery, charcoal, and vegetables. Vessels stopping here must lie well offshore because of the shallow water. A girl in a multi-striped hat (above) plays beside a boat that carries goods ashore from the merchant ships at anchor.

with the first crop of tobacco, and some time in 1625 a French vessel limped in after fighting a Spanish warship. The Caribs posed a threat to the struggling colony, so the English allowed the French company to disembark and establish itself.

Together the Europeans wiped out the Indians, finally driving the remnants off the island, but they did not have long to rejoice. A Spanish fleet attacked in 1629, destroyed the houses and crops, and banished most of the inhabitants.

Some of the refugees sailed downwind to the small island of Tortuga. There they joined outlaws who had been driven from nearby Hispaniola by the Spanish. The settlers earned their living by selling meat to passing vessels. They dried it over fires called *boucans*—giving them the name buccaneers, which lingered long after they had left Tortuga as sea rovers to prey on Spanish shipping. So I like to think that St. Kitts might almost claim another title, "Father of the Pirates."

After the Spanish fleet departed, the St. Kitts colonies were soon re-established, the English taking the center and the French the two ends. From 1639 to 1660 the French part was governed by Philippe de Lonvilliers de Poincy, who built Château de la Montagne, a castle in the European style. There he lived in almost feudal splendor, administering all the French West Indies.

Until destroyed by a terrible earthquake

NATIONAL GEOGRAPHIC PHOTOGRAPHER WINFIELD PARKS

Palms straight as ships' masts circle the clock tower in Basseterre, capital of a new "State in Association with the United Kingdom": St. Christopher, Nevis, and secessionist Anguilla. The town—swept by hurricane in 1843, fire in 1867, flood in 1880—survives as a shipping center.

Roaming the fields of Bayford Estate, a couple climbs away from Basseterre and the coastal plain. I▶

about 1689, when the ground opened nine feet in places and swallowed whole sugar mills, De Poincy's mansion must have been the wonder of the Caribbee world. The fortified château was of brick and cut stone, three stories high, and flanked by gardens watered from a mountain stream. Vivid banners flew above the parapet to celebrate French victories and public holidays, and for special occasions musicians played clarions from the roof.

A surprising amount of the original construction remains. I walked through a cloister supported by arches made of tiny bricks imported from France, a cool sanctuary whose lichen-covered walls had witnessed the pageant of three centuries. I had heard the story that once a tunnel led from the château to St. Peter's Church, more than two miles distant, a secret route which would allow defenders to escape or to surprise a besieging force from the rear. Sure enough, I found the entrance, but before going far inside the tunnel I saw that the way was blocked where the ceiling had collapsed.

Despite its problems, Basseterre has an air of bustle and prosperity, yet without losing its colonial character. In 1672 a Mr. Blome wrote a tourist's-eye view which is

Just out of church, families of cane workers start homeward past sugar fields that stretch for miles. The crop sustains St. Kitts' economy.

e distance looms the cloud-capped cone of Nevis, a daughter colony of St. Kitts settled in the 1600's.

FRED WARD, BLACK STAR (BELOW), AND NATIONAL GEOGRAPHIC PHOTOGRAPHER WINFIELD PARKS

still an almost perfect description. "... A Town of a good bigness, whose Houses are well built, of Brick, Freestone, and Timber; where the Merchants have their Storehouses, and is Inhabited by Tradesmen, and are well served with such Commodities, both for the Back, and Belly, together with Utensils for their Houses, and Plantations, as they have occasion of.... Here is a fair, and large Church, as also a publique-Hall, for the administration of Justice: Here is also a very fair Hospital...."

The focal point of Basseterre is the Circus, a circular park behind the pier. At its center stands a cast-iron monument from the Victorian period—an ornamental structure of columns and iron curlicues topped by four clocks, each facing a different quadrant. On the sidewalk paralleling the black-sand beach there was still a West Indian version of an Oriental bazaar. Some women had set up tables and booths, others had simply spread their goods out on the side-walk. For passers-by they displayed everything from plastic bracelets and bangles stamped out in Manchester or Osaka factories to patiently handcrafted local products: brooms of palm fronds, woven mats of coconut fiber, and clay cooking pots.

On the streets radiating from the Circus, I strolled past show windows of stores stocked not only with "Commodities, both for the Back, and Belly," but also with "Utensils for their Houses" that Mr. Blome could not have imagined—electrical appliances ranging from vacuum cleaners to washing machines. In well-stocked supermarkets I bought frozen food to take back to *Sans Terre*.

The most commanding feature of the leeward coast of St. Kitts is Brimstone Hill, the "Gibraltar of the West Indies." Rising almost vertically more than 750 feet above the plain, the outcropping does resemble the Rock. Carib legend maintains that Brimstone Hill was once part of Mount

Liamuiga — the "Fertile Isle," the Caribs called St. Kitts. Scooping freshly cut sugarcane, a long-armed tractor whisks the stalks into carts for loading on railroad cars. Thirty-six miles of narrow-gauge track take the crop to a mill that converts it into sugar and molasses for export.

Misery, blown out like a giant plug during a volcanic eruption.

When I climbed to the top of Brimstone I saw another reason for the comparison to Gibraltar — an enormous complex of fortifications designed to be impregnable to the weapons of the day. Thick masonry walls towered above the cliffs, and flanking outworks commanded the few possible approaches up the slopes.

As I looked down from the parapets I recalled the words of Lt. Col. Henry Howard, Administrator when St. Kitts had been a Crown Colony, on my visit in 1965. "Military engineers planned Brimstone Hill as a bastion that could never be captured," he had told me. "Oddly enough, the only time it was attacked, by the French in 1782, it fell. While still under construction, it surrendered to the Marquis de Bouillé and 6,000 seasoned French troops. The garrison consisted of 1,200 men, but the odds against them were made even worse by

local hostility. The Kittitians were said to be so infuriated by Admiral Rodney's pillage of the neighboring Dutch island of Statia the year before — when shipping and stores belonging to the St. Kitts merchants were seized together with Dutch property — they refused to help the British carry up cannon and ammunition from the base of the hill. The besieging French captured these and turned them against the defenders, and for nearly a month concentrated cannon and mortar fire on the summit.

"When the garrison finally surrendered, less than half the troops were fit for duty. The French were so impressed by their bravery that they allowed them the full honors of war, and so the English troops marched out carrying their arms, drums beating and colors flying."

In 1783 the fort came back into English possession, but by the time it was completed the need for it had largely vanished. After the Battle of the Saintes, the focus of the military struggle again shifted to Europe. Nevertheless, a garrison remained at the fortress until 1854.

Today Brimstone Hill is comparable to English Harbour, representing the highest development of land fortifications during the same period. Most of the wooden structures have rotted away, but some of the stone battlements are as solid as when the last mason put down his trowel. And time will never destroy one of the world's most magnificent panoramas. Below us, St. Kitts was dwarfed to the scale of a relief map, and beyond blue channels loomed Statia and Saba, our next island goals.

After I descended from Brimstone Hill, my driver showed me where St. Kitts is trying to make a break with its one-crop dependency. We passed through Basseterre and continued along the coastal road to Frigate Bay. To my astonishment, I found one of the most ambitious developments I had seen anywhere in the islands. On a narrow neck of land washed by the Caribbean on the south and the Atlantic on the

147

north, bulldozers and graders were carving roads for an 850-acre community site.

"The master plan calls for 320 plots for small homes," I was told by Clifford Godfrey, director and project manager for Higgs and Hill, Ltd., a subsidiary of an English construction firm. "In addition, there will be 290 'maisonettes,' double or semidetached houses, plus 459 apartments. An 18-hole golf course is being built, and eventually the salt pond will be transformed into a marina, with an outlet to the Caribbean. It is a long-term project, but when completed, Frigate Bay Development will provide a cinema, sports clubs, restaurants, churches—everything a visitor could require in a self-contained community."

Since there is a which-comes-first, the chicken-or-the-egg relationship between developments to accommodate visitors and transportation to bring them from afar, a correlated effort is being made to enlarge the airport. Frequently in my various stops I heard thoughtful islanders mention "jumboitis" as an epidemic disease among political leaders, and undoubtedly many hopes for the future are pinned to ever-growing numbers of tourists. On the basis of what has happened in the past decade, it is probably not a vain hope.

Mr. Godfrey gave me a personal example: "My brother is 61 years old, and he had never really left his doorstep in England. Suddenly last year he ups and decides to see the West Indies. I think there will be more and more like him, especially if the big new jets bring lower fares."

SUNBATHING VISITORS on the beach rimming Frigate Bay will look over historic waters. In 1782 the British and French navies battled just offshore. Although something of a curtain raiser to the Battle of the Saintes, the engagement was described by the naval historian and strategist Capt. Alfred Thayer Mahan in *The Influence of Sea Power upon History* as not only standing in "the very first rank of naval battles," but also as "the most brilliant military effort of the whole war."

When Brimstone Hill was under siege a squadron commanded by British Commodore Sir Samuel Hood rounded Nevis Point on the afternoon of January 24. A numerically superior French fleet under Admiral Comte de Grasse was anchored in Frigate Bay, forming a naval shield to guard against English reinforcements.

When Hood appeared, De Grasse hoisted sail and stood out of the bay in battle formation. But Hood's ships turned away and steered southward, as though retreating. Through the night the French remained on the alert, while Hood kept to windward. Suddenly, the next morning, the English fleet tacked back toward Basseterre. The French, being to leeward, could not cut them off.

De Grasse realized too late what was happening. Hood sailed near the spot De Grasse had vacated, thus putting himself between the French and their shore base, established to assist in the siege of Brimstone Hill. The English ships anchored so they could swing themselves around to reload after each broadside and thus deliver two rounds to the enemy's one.

The French fleet filed past twice, absorbing heavy punishment, but failed to break the British line. De Grasse blockaded the island for nearly a month, then sailed to Martinique to refit his ships. It was this delay which gave Rodney time to arrive from England and take up watch at Pigeon Island, before he pursued and defeated De Grasse in the decisive Battle of the Saintes.

During my stay ashore the weather moderated. Gradually the hardest punch went out of the squalls, and the marching seas in The Narrows subsided. With them diminished my greatest worry. Ahead lay islands of the Netherlands Antilles, Statia and Saba, volcanic cones rising steeply from the depths. Even under normal conditions they can be difficult to approach. Should the swells continue, I would not be able to land.

As though to reassure me, St. Kitts put on a spectacular display as *Sans Terre* departed. The heavy black clouds which had hung over Mount Misery since our arrival began to shred. Like a spotlight the sun moved across the green fields of cane, then illuminated Brimstone Hill, etching each detail into cameo sharpness. A rainbow ran from the uppermost bastion to the mountaintop of Statia. All we had to do was follow, to find the pot of gold.

Royal poinciana unfolds a scarlet umbrella above Brimstone Hill. Across the channel an extinct volcano, The Quill, rises 1,950 feet on the island of Statia, the author's next landfall.

XI *The Dutch Windwards: Statia, Saba, Sint Maarten*

Ruins of once-busy Lower Town remind Statians of their island's role as a trade center in the 18

BEFORE WE ARRIVED off Oranjestad, the rainbow vanished into a sky of depthless blue. But as I looked ashore to the ruins on the beach, I remembered we were too late for the pot of gold, in any case. Rodney had carried it away in 1781.

Sint Eustatius—or Statia, as it is generally called—was once among the busiest ports in the Caribbean. Ships clustered along its narrow bank of soundings, and a stream of lighters and barges shuttled to the beach day and night. Full warehouses built to the water's edge flanked the roistering taverns and sailors' hangouts of Lower Town; in fine homes on the plateau above lived the prosperous merchants of Upper Town.

Declared a free port by the Netherlands, Statia in the 18th century had become the crossroads for trade between Europe and America, and among the islands. Ships from Boston or New York could clear for the Netherlands West Indies with cargoes for English merchants, then meet ships from London or Liverpool loaded with goods desperately needed by the American colonists, including munitions used during the Revolutionary War. Statia became the "Golden Rock," reputedly the wealthiest island of its size in the world.

At the height of its bustle and prosperity,

ntury. The "Golden Rock" reached its peak in 1790 with 8,124 people—six times the population today.

in sailed the American brigantine *Andrew Doria* on November 16, 1776, when the ink was hardly dry on the Declaration of Independence. Rounding to smartly, she dipped her colors, and upon acknowledgment fired a salute to Fort Oranje, capping the hill of Upper Town. There was a pause while Governor Johannes de Graaff made a difficult decision, but then his guns boomed out the first salute by a foreign government to a flag flown by the Continental Navy.

The incident added fuel to the fury of the British Government and its fighting men, but almost five years passed before they could retaliate. Then came a dispatch to Admiral Rodney in Barbados that England had declared war on the Netherlands. Before the islanders received the news, Rodney pounced with his fleet. The first intimation Governor de Graaff had of hostilities was receipt of an ultimatum from Rodney and troop commander Lt. Gen. John Vaughan stating that "we . . . demand the instant surrender of the island of St. Eustatius and its dependencies with every thing in and belonging there to. We give you an hour from the delivery of this message to decide. . . ."

De Graaff began his reply of surrender by writing, "Well knowing the honour and humanity of the two commanders," but his optimism was unfounded. Rodney picked the island clean. He carried away goods worth an estimated $10,000,000, according to the valuation of the time.

Since the system of "prize money" allowed naval officers a share of captured booty, Rodney had a personal interest in the proceedings. He even continued flying the Dutch flag over Fort Oranje for more

First foreign salute to the flag of a warship of the infant United States boomed from Dutch guns on Statia. On November 16, 1776, the *Andrew Doria,* a brigantine of the new Continental Navy, sailed into the harbor below Fort Oranje. After a dipping of colors, the ship fired a salute. The Dutch hesitated, then replied. The incident infuriated the British, and five years later Admiral Rodney sacked Statia. *Finisterre* (below) rolls at anchor in the historic roadstead.

than a month, adding unwary latecomers to the bag until he had captured 150 vessels. Before being driven away by the French after nine months of occupation, Rodney took perhaps 40 more ships in the waters off Saba and Sint Maarten.

When we turned into the wind to anchor, I saw an automobile coming down the road from Upper Town, and before we had swung back on the chain a surfboat was alongside. To my surprise, I recognized an old friend, Gerard van der Wal, Administrator of Saba when I visited there in 1965.

"Welcome!" he called to the flying bridge. "When I saw a gray boat coming in, I knew it had to be you."

Because of the bad weather, I had cabled from Antigua, asking that a surfboat be sent out if there was any possibility of landing at Statia. Now I was glad we had taken the precaution, for we still found a swell running onto the beach of Lower Town which would have swamped our dinghy.

We had no sooner stepped ashore than the dynamic Mr. van der Wal, who was standing in for the vacationing Administrator of Statia, began telling me of the island's projects. "First, we must have ports for ships and a bigger airport for jets," he said in fluent English. "The harbor will be just south of here in Gallows Bay, but it is not yet certain whether we will build a breakwater or a pier. Engineers in Holland are working with a scale model of the island to observe the effect of simulated hurricane seas, before completing the plans."

Signs of renewed life were apparent in Lower Town. The still-solid foundation of a ruined warehouse was being used in building the Golden Era Hotel, which will

PAINTING BY PHILLIPS MELVILLE

Harboring 200 ships at a time, the port of Oranjestad funneled riches to Statia, shipper for the plantation isles and trading center between Europe and America. The old print errs in placing Fort Oranje at sea level. Actually, the fortification stands on the cliffs above the beach. The island's fortunes waned when trading—and even smuggling—declined in the 19th century.

stand almost directly below the ramparts of historic Fort Oranje. Farther away, in a scallop of the black sand beach known as Gallows Bay, oil storage tanks have been built to meet anticipated needs.

In Upper Town government buildings flanking the fort were being remodeled. Seeing the spic-and-span façade of a new post office, I remembered a ritual surviving from sailing-ship days. On my previous visit, investigating a babble of voices, I had found most of the population of Statia on the veranda of the post office, with the overflow spilling into the yard. Above the crowd stood a postal clerk with a sack of mail.

As he extracted each letter he called the name of the addressee in a loud voice: "Daniel Woodley, Albertis Leverock, Carol van Putten, Leo van Zanten . . ." Each name

brought a response: "Here I is!" someone might shout from the back, and the letter would be passed from hand to hand; or a friend might reply, "She home sick. She say if she get a letter she come fetch it tomorrow"; or, "Give it to me. I'll leave it by!"

This took place regularly when the mail plane came only twice a week from Saba and Sint Maarten. "Now we have a 19-passenger de Havilland Twin Otter on a twice-daily schedule from Sint Maarten except for Thursdays," Mr. van der Wal said as we drove toward the airport, on the windward side. "We also have twice-daily flights to St. Kitts four days a week."

More than 8,000 people once lived on Statia. In 1965 the population was 1,214, but Mr. van der Wal told me it had increased to 1,350, due in part to repatriation from

Netherlands flag at Fort Oranje flies above a plaque given by President Franklin D. Roosevelt to commemorate the first foreign salute to a U. S. warship. Obelisk honors Dutch Admiral Michiel de Ruyter.

Curaçao and Aruba, larger islands of the Netherlands Antilles, where automation has cut back the number of oil-refinery jobs.

"Many of our newcomers, whether returned natives or Americans, are retired people. We have to aim for a different kind of tourist than those who go to Puerto Rico or even Sint Maarten—the types who want to relax, not to be running to a casino," he continued as the road wound up aptly named Round Hill.

From the summit we looked down on a scene of rugged beauty. Although not so steep as Saba, nor so dotted with reminders of the colonial era as Nevis, Statia somehow combined both. Seas creamed into coves along the rocky shore. On a flat lay the airstrip. The runway could be extended for jets simply by whittling away a low hill.

For the first time in my experience Statia was green; on each of my previous visits it had been suffering from drought. The arid years reached a climax in 1968, when 60 percent of the cattle died and crops burned in the fields. That year the dry season started in November instead of in January and continued until May—"six long months with barely a drop from the heavens," in the words of an island farmer.

Beyond Round Hill were spread the holdings of former U. S. Army Capt. George A. Bauer and his wife. While stationed in Puerto Rico, the Bauers decided they wished to continue living in the West Indies, so they retired to Statia and put their savings into land for sale as homesites.

"We have sold 83 of 270 lots," I was told by Mrs. Bauer, "more of them in the first

155

Faces glowing with affection, students of S

Ring-around-the-rosy: Waiting for a bus on French St. Martin, smiling schoolgirls drive away boredom with a favorite game.

Follow the leader: St. Martin boys teeter on a palm tree. Later, the salt water of Marigot Bay will soothe sore hands and feet.

All fall down: A winsome water sprite kicks joyfully on the sandy bottom of her natural bubble bath at Zeelandia Beach on Statia.

FRED WARD, BLACK STAR (BELOW), AND TED SPIEGEL, RAPHO GUILLUMETTE

zef School, Saba, present birthday bouquets and their prized paintings inscribed "for our sister."

five months of this year than in all of last year. We're getting a spillover from Sint Maarten, where land is fast becoming scarce and expensive. Our prices run from $6,000 to $16,000 an acre — not so low as when you were last here, but still among the lowest in the West Indies."

I later learned from the Bauers that within seven months after my visit they had sold 107 more lots, and prices had already reached $8,000 to $20,000 an acre.

On our return to Oranjestad, Mr. van der Wal walked with me to a parapet of Fort Oranje. Looking down, we could see bottom through the clear water off the beach. Plainly visible were dark patterns, not coral reefs, but the foundations of warehouses and a seawall. Judging from the ruins, Lower Town must have stretched nearly a mile, a long narrow strip between the sea and the high ground. Turning to look inland toward Upper Town, I could see ruins of brick houses — some with the walls fallen away except for stone-arched windows — and the remains of a church.

Before leaving the fort, we paused before a reminder of how some of Statia's troubles were triggered. At the base of the flagpole in the center of the small parade ground is

a bronze plaque which reads in part: "Here the sovereignty of the U.S.A. was first formally acknowledged to a national vessel by a foreign official. Presented by Franklin Delano Roosevelt, President of the U.S.A."

On my previous visit I had had a surprise at sundown as I prepared to make evening colors aboard *Finisterre*. Dr. Melville Bell Grosvenor of the National Geographic Society was a shipmate. Before coming aboard, Mel had a private talk with the Administrator. So, when we dipped our ensign, we were answered by a salute from the Netherlands flag over Fort Oranje.

The six Dutch islands in the Caribbean are an integral part of the Kingdom of the Netherlands. Three of them — called the "ABC group," for Aruba, Bonaire, and Curaçao — cluster near the coast of Venezuela. Statia, Saba, and Sint Maarten, the "3-S group," lie 500 miles to windward of the ABC group and are therefore to the Dutch the Windward Islands, even though they lie among the British Leewards. Willemstad on Curaçao is the main seat of government, where the legislature elected by the islanders meets, and where the Crown-appointed Governor resides. On Sint Maarten a Lieutenant-Governor, also appointed

157

Lacking beaches or ports, Saba's precipitous slopes plunge to 100-fathom depths only 600 yards offshore

International family of islands became pawns in a prolonged European power struggle. By 1816 Statia alone had changed hands 22 times.

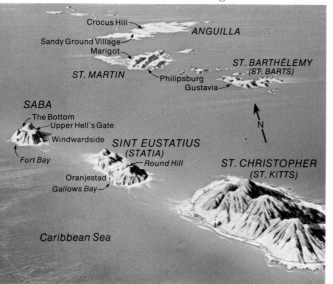

by the Crown, follows the Queen's interests in the Windwards. Satia and Saba have Administrators. On every island an elected council conducts local affairs and serves as a check and balance on the appointed officials.

As *Sans Terre* neared Saba, I felt a stirring of excitement. For me, it has always had a through-the-looking-glass quality. So many legends have evolved around the steep volcanic cone thrusting almost vertically from great depths that it is hard to separate reality from fantasy. The island has always been difficult of access. Even today there is no harbor, so every landing from the sea is a matter of chance, and even hardened aerial voyagers are likely to feel the same about their first descent. Thus Saba has long remained one of the least-known islands of the northeastern Caribbean.

PAINTING BY HEINRICH BERANN, AND N.G.S. PHOTOGRAPHER EMORY KRISTOF

...ettlers defended their island against pirate attacks by tumbling stones upon the heads of invaders.

There were tales of a town called The Bottom, though it stood high on a mountainside; of boats built on the heights and lowered to the water; of The Ladder, precipitous steps cut into a cliff; and of a population so predominantly female that Saba was called "the island of women."

The outline of triangular Saba has been compared to Napoleon's cocked hat. Highest in its crowned center, the island slopes down on three sides. Nowhere could my eye detect a flat spot. Sunshine etched into sharp relief the chasms that fissured the cliffs, bold and forbidding, while surf broke heavily around the base. Jagged peaks tier on tier seemed to form a stairway from water level to the cloud cover, offering no place for man's habitations. I recalled the exclamation of a former shipmate on his first landfall: "I don't see how you could grow anything there but mountain goats!"

Yet the early colonists managed to grow sugarcane, usually a flat-country crop, and gardens high on the slope of the uppermost peak still produce vegetables and fruit. Clinging to the rock sides were white blocks of houses, and, as *Sans Terre* drew close enough for me to make out details, I saw an automobile crawling around a hairpin curve high above. I could also see white water at Fort Bay landing, which offers the only access by road from the sea to the towns above. Since the first jeep road was completed, the tortuous steps of The Ladder have begun to crumble through neglect.

We were not welcomed by the sea gods guarding Saba. Each time Bruno Brown tried to get a loop of line over the hook of a huge steel mooring buoy, *Sans Terre* was tossed away by a vicious series of crests.

159

Finally one flung our bow against the buoy with a sickening crunch. From the wheel, trying to maneuver close enough, but not too close, I wished that officers of the Royal Navy had been given courses in lassoing!

Even when we were secured, our troubles were not over. The surfboat crews were not on duty. I watched a jeep with a single occupant arrive at the landing. After a long wait—which later I learned was in hope of others arriving to help—the lone man began working one of the smaller boats toward the water. How he did it I still do not know, but Stevanis Heiligher launched the craft through the surf, and managed to ship his oars and gather headway before the next crest broke aboard.

When he came alongside, it was like trying to transfer between two elevators going in opposite directions. *Sans Terre* lifted on one swell as the smaller boat plummeted on another, but suddenly both hung poised for an instant and I tumbled aboard.

After I scrambled ashore, only slightly damp from a small sea which broke over the stern as the keel grated on the rocks, Stevanis told me it was the first day in a week that the surf had moderated enough to make a landing possible. The boat crews were not keeping lookout, for they did not expect anybody to arrive.

The slightly topsy-turvy quality of Saba extends to its place-names. Although Dutch is taught in schools and is the language of official documents, English is universally spoken, even in the homes. Occasionally this causes some confusion. In the town of The Bottom, *Kerkstraat* is painted on the signs, but a stranger asking for guidance will be directed to Church Street.

For that matter, naming a town The Bottom when it lies in a bowl-shaped valley some 700 feet above the sea seems illogical by most standards. English travelers must have misunderstood *botte*, a word of Dutch derivation meaning "bowl," and interpreted it as "bottom." However, it was "unanimously resolved" at a public meeting of the inhabitants in 1868 to change the name of The Bottom to the town of Leverock "in token of our Love and Esteem for our most worthy and Excellent Lieutenant-Governor." Apparently the resolution was forgotten. Efforts to change the name of Hell's Gate—origin unknown, for the settlement, often wreathed in clouds, seems much closer to heaven than to hell—also met with no success.

The Bottom had a reassuring sameness, and I would particularly like to see it remain unchanged. Small houses faced narrow streets. Tiny shops displayed lists of produce imported from other islands, with many items scratched out because the weather had made deliveries impossible. The major innovation I saw was a sports park with a high wire fence to keep a loose volleyball or basketball from dribbling itself down the mountainside.

When Gerard van der Wal had finished his term, he was succeeded by the first Negro Administrator in island history, who was also the youngest. Twenty-three-year-old Joseph E. Richardson was chosen by the Netherlands Antilles government in Curaçao to attend three years of special government-administration courses in Holland because of his outstanding work as assistant treasurer of Sint Maarten.

Less than three months before my arrival, Joe Richardson had come to Saba for the first time. "I was born on Sint Maarten," he told me, "and all my life I have been looking at the peaks of Saba, wondering what the island was like. Then when I first stepped ashore, it was as Administrator."

MELVILLE BELL GROSVENOR

A short flight by Dornier 28 (right) and a very crooked road carry visitors from Sint Maarten to Windwardside with speed, comfort, and thrills. Sabans designed and built the tortuous track.

NATIONAL GEOGRAPHIC PHOTOGRAPHER WINFIELD PARKS

Roaring surf pummels nimble boatmen landing cargo at Fort Bay, Saba. For centuries, both freight and fear-numbed passengers reached the isolated island only by this "port of entry." Now visitors land on an airstrip islanders carved from the spur of a mountain.

NATIONAL GEOGRAPHIC PHOTOGRAPHER WINFIELD PARKS

Like an ogre's fastness, fog-shrouded volcanic cliffs rise behind the dollhouse hamlet of Upp

He paused. "I still find it hard to believe."

Obviously he had put his time to good use. After he joined us in Stevanis Heiligher's jeep, Sabans of all ages spoke and waved as we chugged along the road to the town of Windwardside. I could not help contrasting our easy ascent with the laborious climb I had made on my first visit in 1947, when I toiled up a narrow path that frequently turned into long flights of steps. Two porters climbed with me, carrying bedding and food, as the government guesthouse was not staffed. In those days, every item used on the island had to be transported from the sea to the heights on the backs of men or donkeys.

In 1947 the road linking Fort Bay and The Bottom had just been completed. Children taken for their first ride in the Ad-

ministrator's jeep screamed because "the houses went back so fast." Now there are more than six miles of paved road, and 84 vehicles, mostly jeeps, so the old profession of porters is no more.

As we drove, I learned of a development which soon may spell the finish of the surf-boat crews, another island calling handed down through the generations. "Work will begin on the Saba *Havendam* this year," Joe Richardson told me. "It will be an L-shaped breakwater of enormously heavy stones, extending from shore almost due south, with an arm running southwest. Behind it the water should stay calm in any but the worst gales."

Expected to take three years to complete, the sheltered landing ultimately could make a great difference in the island's economy,

One story up, a villager paints his roof with the methodical diligence of a good Netherlander.

Fourteen hundred feet above the Atlantic, ribs of a cabin cruiser meant for tourists frame the Lesley Johnsons of Upper Hell's Gate. For final assembly Johnson planned to carry the boat down—rib by rib—to the water's edge.

ell's Gate, highest of four communities on Saba.

as cruise liners could schedule Saba as a regular stop. "Three small ships came in this year," Joe continued, "but if it is rough they can't land passengers, so they have to cancel. The breakwater will also allow the bigger ships to use their own boats to put people ashore."

A final twist in the road brought us to the town of Windwardside, at last something logically named—it is on the side of the island exposed to the sweep of the trades. Neat white cottages with softly faded red roofs nestled behind white picket fences. No two homes stood on the same level. Wisps of cloud as cool and damp as Nantucket fog blew past, muting the color of flowers and occasionally blotting out the distant glint of the sea, 1,300 feet below.

I have often wondered why inhabitants

Dolores shares her surname, Hassell, the most commonly heard name on the tiny island, with 248 other Sabans.

of the flattest country of Europe chose almost the steepest island of the Caribbean for a new homeland. Dutch settlers arrived about 1640, and though the island changed hands among the English, French, and Dutch 12 times, it was finally returned to the Netherlands on February 21, 1816.

In the early days the vertical slopes were useful for defense. The traveling priest Père Labat, who visited the island in 1701, recounted that in 1689 a French filibuster captain, M. Pinel, was driven off when the Sabans rolled boulders down from wooden stages they had built on the slopes. Again, in 1690, a French frigate was repulsed by a similar hail of stones.

An indication of how Sabans have remained isolated through the centuries is the incidence of two family names. "As far back as you can look in the records you will find the name Johnson," Gerard van der Wal had told me, "and as early as 1677 a James Hassell was mentioned as Vice Commander. In our present population of 1,030, we have 125 Johnsons and 249 Hassells." Joe Richardson assured me the figures remained virtually the same.

"As of January 1, 1969, the population was 1,036, an increase of only six in four years," he said after checking government records.

There was a period when the population declined. In the 1930's, during the lean years of the worldwide depression, there was almost no work on the island. The men left to earn a living. Many served on ships as seamen, officers, and engineers. Others settled in the New York area, where a few were employed in the Brooklyn Navy Yard. Some found jobs in the oil refineries of Curaçao and Aruba. Although most men sent money home to their families, many wives left to join their husbands. Still, the imbalance in population became noticeable enough for Saba to be written about as the "island of women."

The men who left kept a sentimental attachment to their tiny homeland. Many returned to marry childhood sweethearts, sometimes even bringing back the timber to build a home.

High on the mountainside clings Upper Hell's Gate. Some houses have backyards where drying laundry flaps over a precipice that drops a thousand feet to the airport.

Capt. Reuben Simmons, formerly of the Holland-America Line, lives in retirement. His door with stained-glass panels represents his own taste; his career at sea, followed by serene years on Saba, the pattern of life for many men of the island.

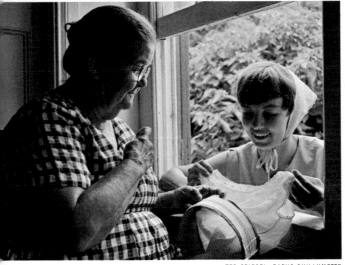

'**Now, pull out another thread . . .**" A Saban artist explains her traditional craft of drawn work to a visitor, who admires an unfinished blouse of so-called "Saba lace" or "Spanish work."

Stopping the jeep, I walked to the edge of the road and peered over.

On first hearing that an airport had been built on Saba, I exclaimed, "Impossible!" I could not remember seeing a piece of flat land larger than a tablecloth. Even now, it seemed a miracle of engineering. I vividly recalled my first landing. Flying from Sint Maarten by Dornier 28, an aircraft designed to climb and descend at very steep angles, I had ridden in the cockpit beside the pilot.

When I had looked down on Saba, the island seemed even more forbidding than when I looked up from the deck of a small vessel. Clouds had gathered over the summit, but lesser crags jutted through trailing streamers of mist. Suddenly the pilot pointed, and below us I saw something that resembled an aircraft carrier's flight deck balanced on a spur of rock, with both ends hanging over the sea. The direction of the wind made a direct approach impossible, so we flew toward a mountainside. At what seemed the last possible moment the pilot banked the plane sharply. When I opened my eyes, the wheels were rolling along the runway. Never had

solid rock felt so reassuring underfoot.

But the road leading down from Upper Hell's Gate is scarcely less impressive as an engineering feat. While the airport was designed by Dutch engineers, the island roads were laid out by Lambert Hassell, a Saban with only elementary schooling. From Fort Bay up to Windwardside and down to the airport, he had plodded along, judging the terrain by eye, planting stakes as he went. Later he had supervised the grading and surfacing. "Every foot was built by man- and donkey-power," I had been told by Gerard van der Wal, "not bulldozers and concrete mixers. Perhaps if Lambert Hassell had taken courses in engineering he would have sat at a desk with a slide rule and said it couldn't be done."

In Windwardside the old customs survive. Every 60 minutes, from seven in the morning until nine at night, a man emerges from the combination post office and police station to strike a bell announcing the hour. Each night at midnight the electricity, turned on at six, goes off after a warning blink, leaving the village in darkness. Few Sabans are awake to notice—they arise

167

Day in port: The Holland-America Line's *Maasdam* moors at Point Blanche on Sint Maarten; passenge

when the sun first shafts over the eastern horizon, and bedtime comes early.

Increasing numbers of visitors arrive by air. Records show 1,781 in 1966; two years later the number had swelled to 3,188. Like Statia, Saba has two daily flights from Sint Maarten, six days a week. Most passengers remain on the island only between morning and evening planes, but those wishing to stay longer can find accommodations. Government guesthouses in both Windwardside and The Bottom welcome visitors, as does a privately owned guesthouse in The Bottom.

At Windwardside a unique inn called the Captain's Quarters had opened since my last visit. The central building was once the home of a retired sea captain. With some astonishment I seated myself on the terrace, and looked across a newly built pool to the horizon. Swimmers feel they are floating in space, for it hangs on the edge of a void. "We have ten rooms, and are open all year," I was told by the co-manager, Charles Thirkield. "Most of our guests are writers, artists, and other professional people who want to get away."

In keeping with Saba's other pixyish qualities, the Captain's Quarters has some unusual rules for guests. "We won't accept reservations for more than two days from people unless they have been in Saba before," Mr. Thirkield said, "or we know they are tranquil, self-sufficient types who will fit into island life. We don't take 'singles' we don't know, because they can be a bore by breaking in on conversations when they get lonely. And we take only second-honeymoon couples—young people on their first honeymoon, we have found, are unhappy unless they can talk to other honeymooners and compare weddings."

When the time came, getting aboard *Sans Terre* was less difficult than landing. Stevanis Heiligher stopped in The Bottom to recruit a crew for a larger surfboat. Before leaving Saba behind, I had one more place I wanted to see, partly out of nostalgia

o ashore to choose luxury goods in Philipsburg.

"I like this one!" A young shopper makes her selection among duty-free watches, sportswear style, in a Philipsburg shop. Jewelry and fine crystal, china, liquors, and tobacco rank as bargains of the town, where visitors, once counted by the score, arrive in thousands.

and partly from curiosity. Prior to jeep days, Ladder Bay had been the favored anchorage; old-time boatmen always told me it was smoother with the wind in the south.

So we found it. Close under The Ladder, the water was so calm we could see a sand bottom fathoms below. On impulse, I decided to anchor. After a sunset of mauve and gold, the night was as quiet as the towering rock itself. As before, on renewed acquaintance, Saba remained shrouded in mist, mystery, and otherworldliness.

Sint Maarten brought us back to the present with a jolt. No other island save perhaps Guadeloupe seemed so astir. From the commercial docks behind Point Blanche to the tourists swarming along Front Street, there was an atmosphere of vitality and urgency. I had heard of "boom towns," but Sint Maarten is a boom island.

Seldom in such a short time and distance have I visited places so different as Saba and Sint Maarten. Their only common denominator seemed that they are both

part of the Netherlands Windward Islands. But not even that applies completely, for the French, since 1648, have shared ownership of the latter. Their part is called St. Martin, honoring the same saint but with a different spelling. Most maps use the French spelling for the island as a whole, and I shall henceforth do the same.

Where Saba is all up and down, St. Martin is relatively flat. Where Saba has no harbors and its "beaches" are slopes of stones, St. Martin has dozens of bays, most of them rimmed by chalk-white sand.

The combination of bays and beaches lures tourists, and government fiscal policies encourage commercial interest. Every graph showing island progress rises steeply. "When you were last here, in 1965, there were approximately 150 hotel rooms on the entire island, counting both the Dutch and French sides," I was told by Julian P. Conner, Director of Tourism. "Visitors who arrive during 1970 will find at least 800 rooms ready for occupancy, and under

169

negotiation or in an advanced planning stage are 2,000 more anticipated by 1975."

Checking sea and air traffic, I found increases to match. In 1958 five cruise ships had put in, in 1965 there were 39, and in 1969 105 made scheduled stops. Airport records told the same story: In 1963 incoming planes numbered 3,752 and carried 13,421 passengers; in '69 there were more than 10,000 landings and 60,000 visitors. Facilities for handling yet greater numbers were under way. A second pier was being built in Great Bay, and the airport terminal enlarged and the runways lengthened.

Another reason for the boom is that both the French and Dutch sides of the island are free of import levies. There are no frontier guards, no customs inspectors, no language barriers, no exchange problems. The banks on the Dutch side will open accounts in any hard currency, even in troy ounces of fine gold, and it is guaranteed that whatever currency is brought in for investment can be taken out in like form. Shops accept cash in any currency.

THE CAPITAL of Sint Maarten is Philipsburg. For centuries it occupied a long sandspit between the ocean and a salt pond that until the turn of the century was the principal source of island income. At high tide seawater was admitted to flat pens created in the lagoon by stone dikes. After sluice gates were closed, the sun went to work and in a few months burned away the moisture until only salt crystals remained. Even the Caribs knew Great Salt Pond; the Indian name for the island was Sualouiga, "the Land of Salt."

Now the very shape of Philipsburg had changed. Huge mechanical shovels had gnawed away part of Fort William Hill, just to the west of the town, and for 18 months a parade of trucks had dumped the fill into Great Salt Pond. Philipsburg no longer was confined to a skinny sandspit, two streets deep. "The extra area of 200,000 square meters [almost 50 acres] will give us space for a shopping center, central government executive offices, and a residential section to cope with our current housing problem," I was told by Reinier Oswald van Delden, Lieutenant-Governor of the Netherlands Windward Islands.

The pace of the Lieutenant-Governor's office reflected the hectic activity outside.

During our interview telephones rang without cease, secretaries scurried past, clerks awaiting a decision hovered at the door. When I remarked that he looked tired, he explained: "Now with the tourist season finished is the time my staff and I can get things done—every morning I'm up at six to be ahead of the telephone."

Mr. van Delden told me of plans that will further alter Sint Maarten. The lagoon occupying much of the low eastern part of the island will be accessible to yachts and small commercial vessels by way of a canal dredged to connect with the sea. "The lagoon will be wholly sheltered in any weather," he commented, "and within we intend to create the most complete and up-to-date yachting center in the Caribbean."

When I asked if more land would be reclaimed from Great Salt Pond, Mr. van Delden sighed. "As soon as we're finished building, undoubtedly the town will be too small again," he answered with a wry smile, "so we'll have to make more plans."

Philipsburg from above has always looked like a ladder. Two thoroughfares running the length of the city form the uprights. Front Street parallels the bay, and Back Street follows the old contour of the salt pond. Short cross streets with Dutch names I could hardly pronounce act as rungs. The new fill is altering that pattern. Although the third main street still had no name, I was assured by a local wag that whatever formal title might be bestowed, residents would refer to it only as "the Other Street." No one had yet tackled the problem of nomenclature should a fourth street evolve!

Front Street was more crammed than ever with shops and shoppers. Goods imported from everywhere would have spilled onto the sidewalk—had there been a sidewalk. In its sleepy early days, the town fathers had not seen the need for such a luxury. Dodging traffic, I looked into stores displaying Danish silver, Swiss watches, English porcelain, Swedish crystal, German cameras, French perfumes, Japanese radios, Italian shoes, Dutch meerschaum pipes, and Scottish sweaters.

Just as there are no barriers against the

Japanese fishermen based on Philipsburg catch yellowfin and albacore tuna and other deep-sea fish off the Dutch Windwards. Frozen fresh, most of the fish go to canneries on Puerto Rico.

"*Le Blanc* is winning!" Fighting cocks clash in a blur of feathers and blood—a spectator sport at Marigot, capital of the French side of St. Martin. Before pitting his highly trained bird, the owner has clipped its wings and fastened gaffs—long, razor-sharp steel blades—to the spurs on its legs.

outside world, there are none between the political divisions of the island. English is commonly spoken throughout the island, so a stranger may go from the Dutch to the French side without realizing it. Driving from Philipsburg to Marigot, capital of French St. Martin, we encountered only a simple marker at the roadside, placed to commemorate three centuries of coexistence, and two signs, one reading Sint Maarten, the other Saint Martin.

Like St. Kitts, the island was settled early by groups from two rival European nations. As on St. Kitts, bickering began and developed into fighting. But unlike the Kittitians, the Dutch and French colonists agreed by treaty to divide the territory.

Legend has it that the division was effected by placing a Dutch soldier and a French soldier back to back at the water's edge, and telling them to walk around the perimeter until they met. A line between the two points would form the boundary, the French getting everything to the north, the Dutch everything to the south. The men started out briskly, but the Dutchman had brought along a flask of Holland gin on the sly. After a few nips he stopped to nap in the shade while the Frenchman plodded along, covering more distance.

Historians offer a different version. They point out that the French colony was strengthened by troops dispatched from St. Kitts. These forced a settlement on March 23, 1648, "by which the island was divided between the two nations, and the equal rights of the inhabitants to the saltponds, chase, fishing waters, dye-woods, minerals, harbours and bays of the island recognized." Regardless of the method of division, the French received 20 square miles of territory and the Dutch 13.

As before, although there is no visible boundary, I found that each section retained its own character. While Marigot's shops sold almost the same range and variety of merchandise displayed in Philipsburg, and at comparable prices, the stores and clerks had remained more in the West

Indian tradition. The sense of urgency and bustle was missing. Instead of being tuned to the busy activity of Juliana Airport and the quayside of Point Blanche, the French capital took its pace from local sloops and schooners bringing produce from neighboring Anguilla. As I strolled among the vendors in the waterfront market, I was reminded of the more leisurely islands lying to the south.

A new pier, providing landing facilities for tourists, may change this. Also, I noted that Marigot had filled in a pond of its own, to build a "*petite Cité Transit, comme Guadeloupe,*" in the words of an inhabitant. Although expansion was not so extensive as in Philipsburg, it was still very evident.

The most startling discovery was a Mediterranean-Creole fishing village planted squarely upon the shores of the Caribbean. From the water the illusion was complete. Even on closer inspection I felt I might be back in the south of France. A narrow lane between stone and pastel stucco houses opened into a village square; following an alleyway beyond, I came upon a tiny cobblestone courtyard which could have existed in Villefranche-sur-Mer. Looking behind heavy wooden doors, I saw rooms with tile floors, timbered beams supporting high ceilings, and wrought-iron railings on balconies reached through French windows. Palms waved against the same sky as the Midi, and beyond lapped water as blue as that of the Côte d'Azur.

The concept of this "La Belle Créole"

173

goes back more than 20 years, and the acquisition of property almost 12. Actual construction has already consumed 4 years. "I didn't want to build a cottage colony or another glass-fronted hotel," I was told by Claudius Charles Philippe, who had created La Belle Créole. An executive for 28 years at the Waldorf-Astoria Hotel in New York, he had become famous as "Philippe of the Waldorf."

While we walked past workmen still hammering and plastering, M. Philippe told me more of his longtime dream. "I wanted to create a village to look like a village and feel like a village, with its own streets and shops, its own roads and waterfront. Yet with it, I wanted to build a hotel in the best French tradition."

WHEN I RETURNED to the Dutch side of the island, the contrast between the two sections seemed more pronounced than ever. Driving to the extremity of the eastern point forming Great Bay, I found a commercial boom to equal the tourist influx. Tucked into a valley near Point Blanche, offices and warehouses stood cheek by jowl in a swirl of dust. But the space was still not great enough. As on so many other islands, bulldozers were biting into the hillside, making room for more buildings. Mounds of cargo unloaded from ships continued to be piled along the road and covered with tarpaulins, for lack of warehouse space.

Alongside the quay lay the mother ship of the fishing fleet, the *Chikuzen*, once Japanese-owned but now the property of the Netherlands Antilles government. Cargo winches rattled as they lifted frozen tuna from small craft called clippers, which resemble whaleship chasers. Slung by their tails, the fish dangled like huge bunches of bananas as they swung through the air.

Crew members climbed from the frigid interiors of the fleet into the blazing sunshine, wearing heavy coats, fur caps, mittens, and thick insulated boots. Hearing shouted orders, I felt I might have been on the pier at Misaki, a fishing port which supplies Tokyo. Forming a frieze along the upper rails of the boats were hundreds of drying sharks' fins and tails, used by the Chinese in making soup.

On this cruise I had again found a shortage of fish in the local markets. A stranger might assume that the converging Atlantic and Caribbean waters would be teeming, but my experience on the net in Martinique had pointed up what I had long known: The inshore waters and reefs have been thinned out by generations of fishermen, and trade-wind seas make it difficult for the fragile gommiers to seek the varieties of the open sea.

The Japanese, ranging far and wide, use the latest techniques to reap a finned harvest. Fishing boats and mother ship are studded with electronic gear: Echo sounders reveal schools far below the surface, and radiotelephones summon other ships to the area of a heavy run.

To learn more of these methods, I called upon George Makimura, managing director of Curaçao Pioneering, N. V. "This year we have 17 clippers, which will take 7,000 to 8,000 tons, working from the Caribbean to the eastern Atlantic. Our catch is mostly albacore and yellowfin tuna," he said. "Only 15 percent goes to Japan and 7 percent to St. Martin and the nearby islands. The rest is shipped to Puerto Rico and Cambridge, Maryland, for canning."

Doodling on a pad, he diagramed the Japanese technique known as long-lining. As a clipper moves ahead at high speed, a double line is paid out astern; flag-capped buoys spaced at intervals keep the upper line from sinking to the bottom. From the lower line Mr. Makimura sketched a seemingly endless row of dangling hooks, with fish rising toward them. The figures he jotted down were startling: "Our 'long line' stretches 40 miles," he said, "and is suspended at depths of about 200 to 330 feet, depending on what the captain thinks best. From it hang between 1,500 and 2,800 baited hooks."

A clipper preceded *Sans Terre* as we left Great Bay. Both of us shaped a course for St. Barts, low on the horizon. Mr. Makimura's words took on added significance as I realized that our companion's fishing line—if the complicated long-line rig could be called by so simple a name—would reach from Philipsburg to Gustavia, our destination, and almost 25 miles beyond.

Languid afternoon at Marigot Bay: A single fisherman moves his boat to deeper water. Starting the outboard and chugging away, he will dodge unmarked shoals in the western harbor.

XII *St. Barts:*
Memories of Sweden

Tiny Gustavia's pocket port dips into the edge of St. Barts. A shopping center for the Caribbea

AFTER ST. MARTIN, the island of St. Barts seemed the embodiment of tranquillity. As we crept into the embrace of a snug harbor, softly weathered red roofs against a green cup of hills reminded me of an earlier Grenada, not yet touched by the pace of the 20th century. The street rimming the waterfront before the shuttered houses bore no traffic. Native schooners, flags drooping, lay alongside Gustavia's town wharf. Echoes sounded from the hillside when our anchor chain rattled down.

Ashore, no one seemed in a hurry. A group of men wearing broad-brimmed straw hats lounged in the shade, gossiping quietly. A vintage automobile coasted down the road and came to rest under a tree, as though it never intended to move again.

Two fishermen sat on the edge of the dock, like carven figures; their cork bobbers did not move, so neither did they.

St. Barts—a contraction of St. Barthélemy—had remained in my memory as one of the most charming of the islands, and I found it so again. Part of the reason is that the town of Gustavia adds a dash of Scandinavia to the smorgasbord of cultures we had already savored.

In 1784 France ceded St. Barts to Sweden in exchange for the right to establish a transshipment center at Göteborg. For almost a century the island remained an outpost of Sweden, far from the skerries of the Baltic.

Remnants of a coaling station and a hospital of imported yellow brick stand opposite Gustavia, named for the Swedish king

e duty-free town sells a variety of wares for less than they cost in the countries that produce them.

NATIONAL GEOGRAPHIC PHOTOGRAPHER JAMES L. STANFIELD

Gustavus III. Although the island was sold back to France in 1877, traces of Scandinavian influence remain in the small windows and scrollwork on many houses. Towheaded children, who would look at home in Sweden, are descendants of the original Norman and Breton settlers.

At Corossol Bay I found a village that might have been lifted bodily from the Brittany coast, allowing for the difference in climate. Although some women went barefoot, many of them wore the traditional pleated and frilled bonnets their ancestors had introduced from France. Strangely, however, a chief occupation of village matrons is weaving hats of straw.

After buying a model favored by local fishermen—one with a wide, upturned brim and a low crown which wedged onto the head to foil sudden puffs—I asked Mme Veuve Emilien Magras to show me how the hats were made. She spoke only French, and I noted she used *veuve* for "widow," in the formal old-country fashion.

Her house stood behind a clump of low palms whose fronds, dried for two weeks in the sun after cutting, formed the raw material for hats and other woven work. The fronds were split into narrow strips, then plaited into bands about an inch wide before being fashioned into hats.

"The village began weaving straw in our grandparents' time," I was told by Mme Pierre Blanchard, Mme Magras's sister-in-law. "Every girl learns how."

The living room and workshop of Mme Magras had a pine floor polished by two generations of bare feet. A flowered curtain hung over the entrance to the bedroom, in place of a door. There was a mirror on one wall, flanked by tinted religious prints and faded family photographs. In one corner dangled a hammock, which could be opened to hang from another hook on the far wall. "It is for when the weather is hot," explained Mme Magras.

As the women worked, chicks followed a clucking hen into the room. Finding other visitors, they departed. Equally decorous were children peeping round-eyed through unscreened, unglassed, and uncurtained

Time stands still for children at play beside a Swedish clock tower. Long ago, a large bell within sounded an alarm when fire broke out.

Fair skin of the people of St. Barts reflects Norman and Breton ancestry, while bare feet and warm smiles hint at a carefree life. A basket weaver carries on traditions of the past century, and frilled bonnets recall the dress of early French settlers.

CARLETON MITCHELL (ABOVE) AND NATIONAL GEOGRAPHIC PHOTOGRAPHER WINFIELD PARKS

In full sunlight, a commemorative crucifix overlooks the harbor at Gustavia; an inscription in French on the face of the cross quotes Christ's commandment to "love one another." On a quiet day, few yachts lie moored. A single car traces hairpin curves of the airport road. Pensive eyes mask the dreams of an island girl (left). Boys (below) lift clawless lobsters from a tidal pool; the author served such langoustes boiled in water scooped from the sea.

windows; although obeying the admonition to be seen and not heard, they were missing nothing of the strange grown-ups displaying interest in something as normal as weaving straw. Beyond their blond heads waved scarlet blossoms of hibiscus and bougainvillea, and drying palm fronds.

A smaller version of St. Martin, St. Barts also has no customs duties, so I stocked *Sans Terre* for our passage to the Virgin Islands. I was amazed by the variety of merchandise, as well as the bargain rates. French delicacies and wines sold for prices hard to believe; even Barbados rum cost less than on the island where it was distilled.

Through Bruno Brown I met another Magras, a merchant named Alexandre. "It is believed that the first Magras arrived from St. Christopher in 1648, as one of a small garrison," he told me as we sat in his office. "The soldiers turned farmers, and sent for their families. Unfortunately, soil depletion gradually made agriculture unprofitable. I opened this store about 15 years ago, and the first tourists came in 1958. This year we had 28 cruise-ship calls, and plenty more yachts than ever before."

Again like St. Martin, St. Barts has a scalloped shoreline, with deeply indented bays cradling white-sand beaches. Before reaching those on the northern coast, we drove past reminders of planter days. In its agricultural years St. Barts overflowed with the bounty of the tropics, growing sugar, cotton, tobacco, and other products. Fences of stone gathered from the fields pattern the hillsides, tokens of intensive cultivation. Tamarind trees abound. The fruit of the tamarind has an acid pulp which is stewed to make jelly; boiled into a syrup, it forms the basis of a cooling punch frequently fortified by the addition of rum, and popular throughout the West Indies.

The landing field on St. Barts, like most others in the Caribbean, has become inadequate. On my 1965 visit, a plane seemed about to dive into the windows of my car as I reached the crest of a hill behind Gustavia. Low-flying pilots had to cut their power just above the road where it crossed the crest, then follow the slope down to the edge of the runway, which stopped short at the sea. Now, I learned, plans to flatten the ridge and improve the airport were already being discussed.

Before I left his store, M. Magras said,

"What is most important to the economy of St. Barts today are the Americans, Canadians, and Frenchmen from Martinique and Guadeloupe, who have bought property and are building homes."

While no incipient suburbia in comparison with burgeoning Pointe-à-Pitre, Gustavia had grown noticeably. Many of the new dwellings are constructed of native volcanic stone. Some stand on sites near the beaches; others perch on hillsides or summits. All have balconies looking over the sea.

ST. BARTS' most famous winter resident is banker David Rockefeller of New York, whose home stands on an isolated point to the west of Gustavia, accessible only from the sea. I was shown through by Nelson W. Aldrich, the architect who designed the house and supervised its construction.

"The house took a year and a half on the drawing board," he said as we walked through rooms of unorthodox shape, "and it was four years building. The basis is a parabola, a shape similar to an ellipse except that the lines never meet—it is as free a mathematical curve as can be achieved. We chose the form partially to funnel the breezes through, taking advantage of nature's air conditioning."

From a terrace which curved around the front of the living-room area, I looked over blue water on both sides of the peninsula. The house seemed to be a continuation of the rocky hillside, its contours and texture blending into the surroundings. Following the modern trend, it was open to light, and offered a breath-taking view.

Quite in contrast was a house on the waterfront, well over two centuries old. I was told it had been the residence of an American appointed as consul in the War of 1812. According to local lore, privateers based on Gustavia during the war had harassed British shipping and rewarded the Swedish free port by bringing back choice bits of plunder.

"You will note that the roof is high-peaked as if to carry the weight of the snows of Sweden," commented my friend Art Hansen as we walked through. "And the same form lets the heat escape. Also, the small windows and thick walls act as insulation. So what worked during a Scandinavian winter isn't bad for a Caribbean summer."

I had first met Art Hansen in St. Thomas in 1947. Even though the islands are no longer a small community where residents and visitors almost invariably know each other, those of us who are old-timers still have a bond of fellowship. Thus he gave me a warm welcome when I appeared at the St. Barts Yacht Club and Hotel, which he had remodeled from one of the oldest houses on the island.

Plaster fallen from a stairwell had revealed gray stone and red bricks bound together by white mortar. When I commented on the lovely combination, I learned one of the unanticipated problems of restoration. "I can't find a sealer which will preserve the effect, yet remain invisible," Art said. "Every time the stereo is turned up, you can see trickles of mortar dust loosened by the vibrations."

Outside stood the mast of a sailing ship, complete with yardarm, which had been made into a flagpole. Conforming to a custom I had observed when cruising Baltic waters, harbor officials displayed the national ensign of each visiting yacht. Among the familiar colors was a flag I did not recognize. Upon inquiry, I found it was flown on behalf of the trimaran anchored in front of *Sans Terre*. The occupant was a Jehovah's Witness missionary from South Africa, northward bound after two years in the jungles of Brazil. Although St. Barts lies off the usual sailing routes, its flag locker must be well stocked.

As before, I found a tidal pool below the Eden Rock Guest House well stocked with a more usual island commodity. From every shaded cavern in a pen of coral rock, long antennae protruded. Two small boys stood by, ready to provide diners with langouste, the clawless lobster of tropic waters. To gourmets who consider the variety inhabiting more northerly latitudes beyond compare, I recommend langouste boiled in seawater until tender—but no longer—served with melted butter, the juice of small green limes, and crushed red peppers.

On leaving the placid harbor of Gustavia, I wondered what our next landfall would bring. For despite conflicting rumors about the reception accorded strangers, I had decided to attempt a visit to Anguilla to see firsthand the island which had declared its independence from St. Kitts, and later from Britain as well.

After measures of reconciliation on the diplomatic level met with no success, Britain sent troops to the island. On March 19, 1969, in Operation Sheepskin, 331 paratroops and marines landed and moved swiftly inland, taking over the airstrip without firing a shot. Soon planes of the Royal Air Force were shuttling from Antigua, bringing in supplies, police, and a detachment of engineers. British Commissioner Anthony Lee arrived to restore the functions of civil government.

The coconut wireless of the islands—rumors true and false that seem to travel as fast as radio transmissions—had already brought word that it was possible to visit Anguilla. There were restrictions, as might be expected in an area under military control, but the island was said to be open to callers. I decided to see for myself.

Exploring the shallows, a finned swimmer snorkels near a reef off St. Barts. Eden Rock Guest House (right) caps a promontory of the rocky isle. In the wide bays that sweep far inland, crescents of white sand embrace pale blue waters.

XIII *The British Virgins and Secessionist Anguilla*

In Deadman Bay, a yawl floats above its own shadow as crew members on Peter Island scrub th

ANGUILLA is supposed to have taken its name from *Anguille*, the French word for eel. The island's shape is certainly appropriate. Sixteen miles long and only a fraction more than three at its widest point, Anguilla may well have the distinction of being girded by more miles of sand than any isle of comparable size in the northeastern Caribbean—where beaches have become pearls almost beyond price.

As *Sans Terre* cruised around the island, Bruno and I looked from the flying bridge into an almost interlocking series of coves, first on the south coast, then on the north, and almost all gleamed powder-white behind multihued shallows of transparent water. Few houses broke the symmetry of the skyline, and, on anchoring among schooners loading salt in Road Bay, I almost forgot why I had come. It was like turning back the clock a quarter of a century, to the West Indies that were.

But the problem of unrest in the present-day world awaited us ashore. As we hauled the dinghy above the tide line, a husky Briton in khaki twill trousers and thick-soled boots strode over. "Good morning, gentlemen," he said politely, but with unmistakable authority, "I am Constable Gibbs. Might I see your passports, please."

We followed him into the shade, where a shortwave field radio crackled. Almost

inghy. Beyond a pipe-organ cactus rises Tortola. Pirates gave palisaded Dead Chest Cay its name.

immediately a Land-Rover drove up, and two men alighted. The leader looked at our passports, too, and then introduced himself: "I'm Detective Sgt. Leslie Barlow, of Special Branch, Scotland Yard."

Politely but firmly he suggested that he would like to visit *Sans Terre*. When he had looked through the cabins—to make sure we were not smuggling arms, we were told later—we were given authorization to remain for three days.

Following the introductory formalities, we had the freedom of the island. A Royal Engineers truck driver offered us a ride to the airport, where we could hire a taxi. Everywhere we were treated with courtesy and friendliness, both by the Anguillans and the occupying forces—and there was no visible animosity between the two.

But there was no mistaking who was in charge. London bobbies stood watch at the piers; the Royal Air Force had set up a control tower at the airport; combat engineers were building a much-needed cargo wharf; a detachment of paratroops remained discreetly encamped behind a secluded beach. The communications network extended to every point.

Against the martial background the Anguillans went about their normal lives. "Anguilla has always been a very poor island," I was told by Emile Gumbs, whose family had lived there since a soldier ancestor sent out during the era of French-English wars had turned settler. "Slaves got along with their masters better than elsewhere; poverty was probably the binding factor. Our major industries now are salt 'picking' and lobster fishing. A large number of our men leave as sailors. More than a thousand work on St. Thomas as teachers, taxi drivers, construction laborers, hotel employees. They send back money to their families. Thus we are largely a remittance economy."

Behind Sandy Ground Village the salt pond ranges in color from delicate pink to deep rose. When evaporation occurs in

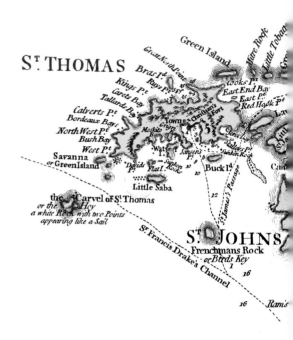

Notorious haunt of Caribbean freebooters, the Virgin Islands sprinkle an English map of 1797. Pirates—like those intent on a division of booty in Howard Pyle's painting—found refuge among the maze of cays and hidden inlets. Today Britain administers most of the group northeast of old St. Johns, and the United States supervises the islands to the west and south.

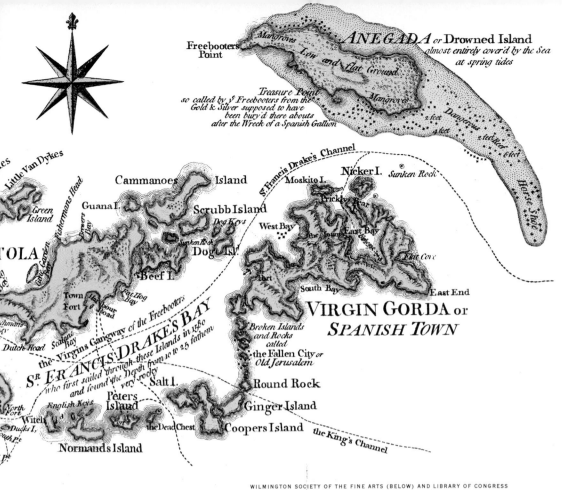

ANEGADA or Drowned Island
almost entirely cover'd by the Sea
at spring tides

Freebooters
Point

Mangroves

Low and flat Ground

Mangroves

Treasure Point
so called by y.ᵉ Freebooters from the
Gold & Silver supposed to have
been bury'd there abouts
after the Wreck of a Spanish Galleon

Horse Shoe

Dangerous
2 feet
4 feet
2 feet Reef
6 feet

Little Van Dykes

Green Island

Cammanoes Island

Guana I.

Scrubb Island

Dog Keys

Fishermans Head

Brewers Bay

Sunken Rock

Dog Isl.

Beef I.

West Bay

S.ᵗ Francis Drake's Channel

Moskito I.

Nicker I.

Sunken Rock

Prickly Pear

the Round Rock

East Bay

Flat Cove

TOLA

Town Fort

Fat Hog Bay

Harbour Road

the Virgins Gangway of the Freebooters

Fort

South Bay

East End

S.ᵗ FRANCIS DRAKE'S BAY
who first sailed through these Islands in 1580
and found the Depth from 10 to 25 fathom
very rocky

VIRGIN GORDA or
SPANISH TOWN

Dutch Head

Scalane Bay

Chmans

North Fort

English Keys

Salt I.

Peters Island

Witch

Fort

the Dead Chest

Normands Island

Broken Islands
and Rocks
called
the Fallen City or
Old Jerusalem

Round Rock

Ginger Island

Coopers Island

the King's Channel

seawater admitted by dikes, and the density of the water increases, reddish algae appear in the brine. From the hill above, where goats grazed, the view was spectacular: the blue and green shallows of Road Bay to the west, a strip of white sand forming an almost perfect half-circle, and, within the pond, mirror-smooth lavender-pink water reflecting trade-wind clouds.

Geologically, Anguilla is formed of coral encrusted on volcanic debris. Besides being long and narrow, it is flat. The greatest elevation is slightly above 225 feet, at Crocus Hill, not far from The Valley, the island's principal settlement, which is more a rambling collection of houses than it is a town. Rainfall is meager, but sufficient produce for export to St. Martin is grown in the rich bottomlands. Unmistakably, Anguillans have remained wedded to the soil and the sea, as were their forefathers before them.

Why should such an outwardly peaceful island have erupted into rebellion so soon after St. Kitts-Nevis-Anguilla became an Associated State? Basically, the Anguillans refused to remain under the central government at Basseterre, St. Kitts. Rallying behind a local leader, Ronald Webster, the Anguillans rejected St. Kitts. Then, only a few weeks later, when the Anguillans declared total independence, it was Britain's turn to react.

"People ask why troops came in," said Major Lewis Huelin of Britain's Army Strategic Command. "Our mission was to install lawful civil authority and to promote a climate of peace and security in which a Caribbean Commission could meet to find a settlement that would be acceptable to all. The British Government does not intend to

Startling as a pirate raid, change comes at long last to Road Town, Tortola, capital of the British Virgins. Below Mount Manuel, landfill rings tiny Wickhams Cay; government funds supplement private finance for two other fill projects. Beyond Burt Point, Sir Francis Drake Channel sweeps past Tortola. Across the channel *Sans Terre* (below) finds a mooring at Peter Island.

force the Anguillans under an administration they do not want, nor does it wish to see a fragmentation of the West Indies into small states."

On leaving Anguilla I noted that for the first time since Grenada the rim of the horizon was unbroken. *Sans Terre* was crossing the Anegada Passage, the widest gap between the island stepping-stones. Soon, however, low shapes began to appear over the bow, until they looked like scattered pebbles. When Columbus found the same cluster of peaks, they seemed so numerous they reminded him of the legend of St. Ursula and the Eleven Thousand Virgins.

Ursula was a British princess who begged her father to allow her to go on a cruise to avoid becoming the wife of a pagan king. She invited ten maidens to accompany her, but others implored her to include them.

When she finally sailed, it took 11 ships of her father's navy to transport the 11,000 young women who signed on.

For three years, the legend goes, they roamed the seas. On the day they disembarked at Cologne, the Huns sacked the city, slaying Ursula and all her companions. Columbus immortalized the maidens when he named the archipelago *Las Vírgenes*.

As in *Finisterre*, I chose to come on soundings through the Round Rock Passage. Islets and rocks stretched away on either beam. To starboard, the ample contours of Virgin Gorda, the "Fat Virgin," rose above a fringe of lesser cays; to port lay a string of smaller jewels: Ginger and Carval Rock, Cooper and Salt, Dead Chest and Peter.

Columbus had dispatched a force of caravels through the same opening, and they had reported "a main large sea having

189

Palm fronds feather a pool on Virgin Gorda, where sun-seeking families wade still water wall

in it innumerable islands, marvellously differing from one another." But the "main large sea," in reality a wide lane of deep water between the Atlantic and Caribbean, takes its name from someone else.

For me it is a unique channel, best described by the *New Sailing Directions for the Caribbee Islands* — the yellowed, brittle pages of the edition of 1818: "Happily . . . nature has arranged [the islands] as to form a grand basin, in the midst, wherein ships may lie at anchor, landlocked, and sheltered from every wind. This basin, or harbour, is the finest that can be imagined, and is called Sir Francis Drake's Bay or Channel; it having been entered by that commander in 1580 [1585], when he proceeded against St. Domingo."

Before going to Road Town, on Tortola Island, the administrative center of the British Virgin Islands, we decided to anchor for a swim off the tip of Virgin Gorda. On the way, we passed a strange formation,

where a prank of nature had dumped huge squarish boulders on a low cay, then tumbled them about. The spot had reminded some unknown early navigator of a ruined city, and it remains on most charts to this day as Fallen Jerusalem.

It was well we had stopped for a relaxing swim, because at Road Town I found a totally unexpected bustle. I had first known Road Town as a tiny settlement. The hillsides had been patterned by vegetable plots and dotted with grazing goats. Children had splashed among anchored sloops, and piles of conch shells alternated with dinghies being built under the palms.

Now Road Town had grown up the hillsides and spread out along the shore. Diesel ferries bound for St. John and St. Thomas, in United States territory, hurried in and out, punctuated by a sleek hydrofoil, its hull rising from the water as it gathered speed. At the head of the pier waited air-conditioned taxis painted in gaudy colors.

om Spring Bay by massive boulders of granite.

Rocks three stories high seclude beachcombers gathering shells in The Baths of Virgin Gorda —a labyrinth sculptured by wind and wave.

One corner of the harbor was crowded with a cluster of yachts. The whole aspect of the town was changing as dredges filled in the waterfront to create additional land and a cargo wharf took shape. The Road Town I first knew lacked people more than it lacked space.

When I scanned the chart of the harbor, I found a whole cay had disappeared. "Wickhams Cay fill is a private development," Acting Administrator Willoughby H. Thompson told me. "It will give us needed space for a decent commercial and shopping area. Later projects financed in part by the government include additional fills and a deepwater wharf, where cruise ships can discharge passengers."

The British Virgin Islands remain a dependency, but under a constitution liberalized two years ago. The Crown-appointed Administrator invites the leader of the party with the most votes in a popular election to become Chief Minister. The Chief Minister then selects ministers to serve under him. "It is really a 'cabinet government,'" continued Mr. Thompson. "We are grappling, struggling, to cope with the problem of suddenly being projected into the modern age."

In February 1966 a bridge connecting Tortola with nearby Beef Island was formally opened by Queen Elizabeth II. The hard-surfacing of the airport on Beef Island had been finished by the Royal Engineers just a few weeks before our arrival.

The British share of the Virgin Islands consists of more than sixty islands, islets, rocks, and cays having a total population

VIRGIN ISLANDS

N

Atlantic Ocean

GUANA ISLAND

TORTOLA

JOST VAN DYKE

GREAT TOBAGO

Pull and be Damn' Point

Great Harbour

Road Bay

Road Town

Sir Fran D Ch

PET ISLAI

Maho Bay

Cinnamed Bay

Caneel Bay

Cruz Bay

Pillsbury Sound

ST. JOHN

NORMAN ISLAND

ST. THOMAS

Charlotte Amalie

"Collection of delights," the author calls the Virgin Islands, praising their "pleasant anchorages, splendid weather with nearly ideal sailing conditions, clear water and simple pilotage." Off the map above lies St. Croix, largest of the American group; yachtsmen reach it by an easy run of 35 miles south from St. Thomas. But throughout the isles sailors watch for shoals, ledges of coral, scattered rocks. Horse Shoe Reef, a coral arc that stretches more than ten miles in a main passage between the Atlantic and the Caribbean, has sent hundreds of ships to the bottom. In 1929 it claimed the freighter *Rocas;* at left, a snorkeler examines her macabre cargo—animal bones bound for a fertilizer factory. At right, the author surfaces with a coral-encrusted cannonball that went down with a British frigate more than 150 years ago.

PAINTING BY HEINRICH BERANN; TED SPIEGEL, RAPHO GUILLUMETTE (LEFT), AND MELVILLE BELL GROSVENOR

estimated at 10,500, with almost 9,000 concentrated on Tortola. It was only on Tortola that I found major change; elsewhere there is still a refreshing lack of clutter. One of the things I find particularly fascinating about Virgin Islands cruising is that a deserted anchorage almost always lies around the next headland from a settlement.

Thus, not many minutes after leaving Road Town, we came to rest again, this time in Deadman Bay on Peter Island, the kind of setting a man might dream about when sleet rattles against the windowpane. A patchwork of pale green and blue shallows lay embraced by a curved arm of white sand, backed by towering coconut palms. Conning our way in by watching the bottom through the limpid water, we dropped anchor. Looking about, I had a vivid memory of my last cruise, when we lay in the same place aboard *Finisterre*. Standing in the shallows, our crew had scrubbed the accumulation of marine growth from the hull. Later came long sessions of water-skiing and snorkeling.

Our nearest neighbor was a bleak little cay named Dead Chest. There, tradition holds, the pirate Blackbeard marooned a mutinous crew, inspiring Robert Louis Stevenson's chant in *Treasure Island:*

> *Fifteen men on the dead man's chest —*
> *Yo-ho-ho, and a bottle of rum!*

Eastward of Peter Island the treasure chest spilled out into islands and anchorages, beckoning us to choose. Our first sampling was The Baths of Virgin Gorda. Along the shore were piled granite boulders, many as high as three-story houses, strewn as a child might scatter marbles. Some were pointed like church spires, others were neatly squared; one great circular boulder balanced atop another like a huge poker chip.

Crawling through a labyrinth of tunnels, we came to a pool. The Baths have been compared to Capri's Blue Grotto because the principal source of illumination is sunshine being reflected through an opening from the sea. Patterns of light shimmered on the huge stones, while an unearthly green glow tinted our bodies as we swam.

Following the shore of Virgin Gorda to the north, we came to Laurance S. Rockefeller's development at Little Dix Bay. "We have grown to 66 units," I was told by

193

In a sparkling breeze, the schooner *Southwind* reaches toward Sir Francis Drake Channel past the peaked roofs of the dining pavilion at Little Dix Bay resort on a Virgin Gorda beach.

Laurance S. Rockefeller, a Trustee of the National Geographic Society, opened the retreat in 1964, giving new life to the island's economy. Below, a young couple samples conch salad

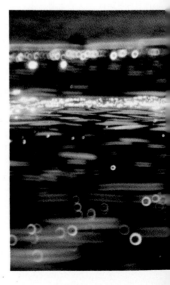

and lobster, fresh from local waters and prepared by a Swiss chef. A visitor lazes on a water wing, awash in an agate bay. Varied sports and a simple quest for quiet lure guests from afar.

Reimar Steffen, then executive assistant manager. From our car we looked down at a central restaurant-lounge surrounded by cottages tucked among the palms. In 1970, I learned, a yacht harbor with space for a hundred vessels would be opened at nearby St. Thomas Bay.

On my 1965 visit the Little Dix employees had been largely European, but now I found islanders. I knew that Mr. Rockefeller wanted to create local employment, yet when he built a hotel most of Virgin Gorda's 800 native residents had never seen a tablecloth. "All were trained here," said Mr. Steffen. "The waiters begin as busboys when they are 16 to 18 years old."

Part of the charm of Little Dix Bay is its location on a beach protected by a coral reef with only a single narrow opening. The lagoon invites lazy swimming in almost any weather. But not far away lie less friendly coral formations, part of the deadly trap of the Anegada Passage.

While it does not take much imagination to visualize the square-rigged ships of buccaneer and honest merchantman alike scudding through the channels of the Virgin Islands, my greatest feeling of association with the vessels of the past has come from seeing and touching their remains in their coral tombs. So with my friend Paul West I sallied forth from Gorda Sound to explore one of the most dangerous graveyards of ships anywhere in the seven seas, the reef lying between Anegada Island and Virgin Gorda.

"Horse Shoe Reef rises above the surface in only a few places," Paul reminded me as we picked our way through shallows. "During darkness or in bad weather, it is invisible until a ship crossing Anegada Passage finds herself in the breakers, unable to escape. More than 300 vessels have left their bones here."

Except for the pale color of the water, and a few spikes of coral barely breaking the surface, we seemed to be anchoring in open ocean. Putting on swim fins and a face mask, I followed Paul over the side. As always, when diving on a tropic reef, I felt I was entering a fairyland. Below, an underwater garden was filled with colors and forms more brilliant and fantastic than anything I have seen on land.

Suddenly Paul swam into view. He pointed and continued on down. A former U. S.

Unspoiled, but uneasy, Anguilla lies 70 miles east of Virgin Gorda, 70 miles northwest of St. Kitts; she refused to remain a "colony" of the latter in 1967, repudiating a role in the new Associated State of St. Kitts-Nevis-Anguilla. In 1969 Anguillans declared their independence; a British force occupied the island; a British commissioner now governs it. Life goes on quietly. At left, boys frolic on a pier at Sandy Ground Village, which curves by Road Bay (below). The photographer calls this "the most beautiful little Caribbean settlement I've seen."

NATIONAL GEOGRAPHIC PHOTOGRAPHER JAMES L. STANFIELD

Navy submariner who was drawn to the Virgin Islands by its wonders below the surface, Paul sometimes seems to me more fish than man. Taking a deep breath, I followed in the wake of his flippers.

Strewn across a patch of sand, surrounded by sea fans and coral, were outlines of muzzle-loading cannon. It was most probably the wreck of an English frigate of the late 18th or early 19th century, traced by the broad arrow of British naval ordnance stamped into each barrel. Between the criss-crossed guns were scattered round objects which I recognized as cannonballs even through their coral encrustations.

On my previous visit, lungs aching for lack of air, I had made a final lunge to seize the nearest sphere and managed to get it to the surface. This time, I was content simply to look, and wonder what combination of circumstances had brought ship and crew to this final resting place, so far from home.

But it was the next wreck which really gripped the imagination. Paul said to me with a grin, "This is the spooky one—the *Rocas,* which broke up on the reef during a storm in 1929."

From the surface, the *Rocas* seemed almost intact. I could see chain, winches, even cargo booms. But then I realized I could also see her boilers and an engine, standing upright as though ready to continue the voyage—a weird X ray view of a ship. Her bow hung on a ledge, so that the stem protruded like a pinnacle of coral, but the hull sloped downward till the stern was submerged some ten fathoms.

Then I saw clearly what made the *Rocas* a spooky ship, an undersea version of a haunted house. Around her shattered sides, bones carpeted the sea floor—thousands of bones. I knew that the huge jaws and teeth were of horses and not of humans. My imagination sped to the sharks that such a cargo would attract.

I had envisioned the scene: the *Rocas* striking the reef, passengers and crew abandoning ship, the horses whinnying in terror as the sharks moved in. But Paul had told me that the cargo was not so grisly as it might seem. "The *Rocas* carried no living animals, only bones to be converted to phosphates. Otherwise, sharks would have carried away the carcasses and nothing would remain." Even with this explanation the spooky feeling persisted.

But the sharks are real. Paul told me he had never speared a fish near the *Rocas* without the wolves of the sea appearing. Before, he had taught me his antishark scream, rather like the rebel yell of the Confederacy. It had a dual purpose—to warn other swimmers and to turn the brutes. Paul had given a sudden yell and I had broken all Olympic swimming records returning to the boat. This time he handed me a more tangible weapon, an eight-shot .44-caliber magnum "powerhead."

"You can ride shotgun," he said casually. "If a shark attacks, jab the barrel hard against him to work the firing pin. Go for the head, near the eyes or jaws."

My knees didn't seem to be functioning right as I swam alongside Paul to the deep water at the stern of the *Rocas*. Below us forms were indistinct. I realized that a shark could materialize from behind a boiler and be on us before we knew it. Undeterred, Paul dove, descending until I could see nothing but his flippers. When he surfaced, I saw a shark. Then a second. And Paul pointed to a third before diving again. He disappeared into a cave formed by twisted steel plating. When he came out he had a grouper impaled on his spear.

As we swam, we both kept watch behind. One shark had gone away; the remaining pair trailed the flapping fish, but stayed near the bottom. Back aboard the boat, Paul stripped off his gear and commented casually, "It's interesting to stay in the water when you see a shark—to observe its behavior." I thought the word "interesting" the understatement of the year.

I T IS ON THE BRITISH SIDE of the archipelago that most cruisers spend their time. While the American share includes the larger and more populous islands of St. John, St. Croix, and St. Thomas, the area to the north and east is splintered. On succeeding days *Sans Terre* poked into a number of anchorages, each different, each with its own charm.

There was Gorda Sound, where the fleet of Sir Francis Drake had rested before attacking Hispaniola. We swung lazily off the Bitter End, a cottage resort built by my old Bahamian friend Basil Symonette to provide amenities for wandering mar-

iners and vacationists; in nautical parlance the bitter end of a line is its ultimate extremity—which applies, because beyond Basil's anchorage little awaited except Horse Shoe Reef and Anegada Passage.

To the north of Tortola lay Guana Island, which takes its name from a rock formation that resembles in silhouette the head of the giant lizard called iguana. Here Louis and Beth Bigelow have created a guesthouse on the ruins of a mansion built by an 18th-century Quaker settler. Beyond, the sanctuary of Great Harbour welcomed us to mountainous Jost Van Dyke. Once noted for its cattle, it also was cultivated by Quakers. From Great Harbour we went by dinghy to two fine beaches, reaching one after rounding picturesquely named Pull and be Damn' Point.

Backtracking, we came to our surprise upon the French tricolor flying below the Union Jack at Trellis Bay, on Beef Island. That night we dined at Le Bistro Français, and next morning rounded Tortola to run the gantlet of Sir Francis Drake Channel. We paused at Salt Island, where salt is still "reaped" by the ancient method of evaporation of seawater admitted to ponds; Little Harbour on Peter Island, the snug cove owned by Percy Chubb, former Commodore of the New York Yacht Club; and Norman Island, whose caves are said to have yielded part of a pirate's treasure.

As *Sans Terre* continued westward, crossing from British to United States territorial waters, I recalled a conversation with Mr. Rockefeller on a previous crossing. "Geographically, culturally, and economically, the two groups are closely interrelated," he had said. "The people trade back and forth, and travel between to find work. Both use the U. S. dollar as currency. Yachts and planes are constantly shuttling tourists—despite all the bother of 'going foreign' each time anyone uses a port of entry. The British and American Virgins are the greatest resort combination in the world, and I hope a way can be found to make their ties even closer in the future."

Small house on a small island defines Anguillan life. With about 5,000 people on 35 square miles, the island exports lobsters, salt from a seawater pond, and men—who work elsewhere and send money home to their families.

XIV *The U.S. Virgins:*
West Indies in Miniature

Cane yielded wealth at the Annaberg Plantation factory on the north shore of St. John in the ear

IN RETROSPECT, I think of the three Virgin Islands that are United States territory as a microcosm, a miniature of the West Indies as a whole. There is St. John, offering escape and seclusion; St. Croix, a vivid reminder of planter days; and St. Thomas, very much in the present. Yet each has characteristics of the others—donkeys plodding as jets flash above, wilderness next to urbanization, leisure alongside bustle, romance and history and progress all mixed together.

Entering Pillsbury Sound, I looked to port and saw St. Thomas. Houses were scattered everywhere on the hillsides; subdivisions patterned the promontories; the ranch-style dwellings that are the stamp of 20th-century America were mushrooming into suburban communities.

To starboard, St. John lay green and unspoiled. I had run along much of the south coast without seeing a dwelling, and now over the bow opened Cruz Bay, a typical West Indian village, and the island's port of entry. A toy fortress on a point,

built in the 17th century during the time of Danish occupation, stood guard over a snug harbor. Boats clustered off the wharf.

I landed and soon was climbing a hill above Maho Bay. In the distance were the peaks of St. Thomas, and around me the wooded slopes of St. John. But as a woman with a hibiscus blossom in her hair appeared, followed by a peacock in full plumage, I felt I might have wandered into a tropic Garden of Eden.

I had come to renew my acquaintance with "Grandma McCully," Ethel Walbridge McCully, who had found what many seek.

"It was a case of love at first sight," she reminded me. "I had come from New York on a vacation in the winter of 1948. In St. Thomas I bought a ticket on a boat going to Tortola. When we passed this bay, I didn't want to go any farther. I asked the captain to put me ashore, but he said his clearance papers didn't permit him to touch American soil again. So I said, 'Let me off on that rock and I'll swim.'"

Eventually Mrs. McCully bought land

800's, but estate and industry had sunk to ruin before 1917, when the U. S. bought the Danish Indies.

NATIONAL GEOGRAPHIC PHOTOGRAPHER JAMES L. STANFIELD

and built her dream house, Island Fancy. Her adventures inspired a book, *Grandma Raised the Roof*, which she dedicated to her seventh grandchild.

As we relaxed on the veranda, Grandma showed me a tile inscribed with her philosophy of life: "How beautiful it is to do nothing, and after doing nothing, to rest." Although this might not be a fitting motto for St. Croix and bustling St. Thomas, it is apt for St. John. And, happily enough, St. John is likely to remain much as it is today, largely because of the foresight and generosity of one individual.

In 1952 Laurance S. Rockefeller arrived for a visit, and quickly decided the island was too lovely to be transformed by civilization. Through Jackson Hole Preserve, Inc., a conservation organization, his representatives bought land, until in 1956 he was able to offer more than 5,000 acres to the people of the United States. The resulting Virgin Islands National Park has since tripled in size, and now includes three-fourths of the island and much of its offshore waters.

"In 1962 we extended our boundaries to take in 5,650 acres of ocean floor," William Bromberg, the park superintendent, told me. "Off the coasts we have ranger-patrolled areas up to a mile out. Spearfishing and the taking of marine specimens are not allowed. It is equally important to preserve unspoiled a part of St. John's underwater heritage."

St. John is as rich in history as in the charms of nature. When the Danes arrived in the mid-17th century, looking for farmland, they found St. Thomas and St. John uninhabited. Shortly after establishing a colony on St. Thomas, some settlers moved to St. John, but the British on Tortola drove them off. In 1716 the Danes tried again, and were allowed to remain.

By 1733, St. John had 109 estates planted in cotton and cane, and 1,295 inhabitants, with slaves outnumbering the planters more than five to one. The future seemed bright. But then came a summer of drought,

Carnival reaches high tide in Charlotte Amalie with a Saturday parade for adults, near the end of a spirited week. A pre-Lenten festival elsewhere, Carnival falls late in April in the Virgin Islands; originally it followed the cane harvest.

NATIONAL GEOGRAPHIC PHOTOGRAPHER JAMES L. STANFIELD

Intricate as rigging for ships of a bygone day, a maze of pipes and towers marks the refinery of Hess Oil Virgin Islands Corp. on St. Croix. Crude oil comes from Venezuela, Africa, and the Middle East; gasoline, butane, and other products go to the United States and abroad.

a plague of insects, and a hurricane. Then measures were imposed to prevent slave runaways and to prohibit dancing and feasting. The slaves revolted. Entering Fredericksvaern with bundles of firewood, the leaders whipped out hidden cane knives, massacred the soldiers, and fired two shots, signal for the slaughter of the planters and the burning of the mills.

Planter families that survived retreated to the Duerloo plantation—now called Caneel Bay—and eventually escaped to St. Thomas. For six months the slaves held St. John. It took French soldiers from Martinique to quell the uprising. Later, many of the estates were rebuilt, but after Denmark abolished slavery in 1848 fields and houses gradually were abandoned, and forest crept back over all.

The Virgin Islands National Park, which received 126,600 visitors in 1970, encompasses reminders of the past ranging from a sugar mill on the Annaberg Plantation, where every step in the making of muscovado may be followed, to Indian petroglyphs under a waterfall near the south shore. Resting with Park Ranger Noble Samuel after tramping two miles down rough Reef Bay Trail, I peered at weird figures carved on lichen-speckled rocks—little men with oval faces, circles for eyes and deeper holes for pupils, big ears, and antenna-like growths on their heads.

The park includes several magnificent beaches, and the Cinnamon Bay campground permits inexpensive enjoyment of the island from tents and simple cottages. In the future the camp will be managed by Mr. Rockefeller's organization, which also operates Caneel Bay Plantation in a more luxurious style. Here two dining rooms open to the sea air serve guests from 130 beach-view rooms.

St. John is a place to drowse and dream, to walk in the woods and to swim off deserted beaches. There is an atmosphere almost predating the colonial era, of an island still awaiting discovery.

By contrast St. Croix is an island still bearing the stamp of its planter tradition. On arriving in Christiansted I strolled sidewalks of brick or cut stone, my steps echoing in arcades formed by pillars and arches supporting balconies above. So perfectly preserved is the heart of the old Danish capital that much of it has been designated a national historic site. I seemed alone with the ghosts of sentries who had paced the walls of Christiansvaern, which looks more like a confection of sugar than a fortification built to ward off pirates as well as the king's enemies.

Driving along Centerline Road, the main thoroughfare of St. Croix, I found other tangible reminders of the West Indies of yore. Not even Nevis has so many surviving monuments. Windmill towers stand on both sides, close to the remains of great houses. I remembered that the island had reached the peak of its wealth about 1796, when 114 windmills and 144 treadmills powered by mules or oxen ground the cane that was the basis of prosperity.

Old prints show teams of six oxen pulling huge high-wheeled wagons loaded with hogsheads of muscovado to sailing ships waiting off King's Wharf in Christiansted. In those times a waving green sea of cane stalks ran down to melt into the blue of the Caribbean, and many families enjoyed a life comparable to that of Europe's aristocracy. Carriages bore ladies along Centerline Road in the shade of palms, while planters and overseers on prancing horses reined in to exchange greetings.

Against such a background, modern St. Croix has amazing diversity. The eastern end is a virtual desert. Cactus shapes and thorny acacias stand stark against the sky, and bosun birds ride the hot updrafts. Less than ten miles to the west, beyond the fields which once were the sugarbowl, the upper slopes of Mount Eagle and Blue Mountain lift steeply above 1,000 feet. Leaving the car, I walked through thick forest, under primeval trees bearded by moss and festooned by air plants and vines.

On the south coast, within sight of Centerline Road, rises an industrial complex. Among the plants stands Harvey Alumina Virgin Islands, Inc., where bauxite is converted into alumina, the white powder that is the raw material of aluminum. There I talked with Russell Sunderlin, general manager. "This is a very highly automated plant," he told me as we entered a room banked by computers, dials, switches, and knobs. "All the basic controls of the processes throughout this 100-acre plant are conducted from this one room, by one man."

Donald Mangaroo, as he paced up and down, answered my questions. A bearded young man in a blue-denim shirt, he typified a new breed of West Indian. "I was born in Jamaica," he said as teleprinters clattered endless streams of numbers, buzzers called attention to changes in temperature or pressure at some distant valve, and lights flashed. "I've been in Central Control six weeks now, and I find the work challenging; it's true that the computers do the

205

Sleek yachts find anchorage and vacationists find congenial fellow guests at Caneel Bay Plantation, a nonprofit resort established by conservationist Laurance S. Rockefeller. In 1956 he gave the first 5,000 acres for the park that now covers much of St. John and its offshore waters.

assembly. Ten plants on St. Croix and four on St. Thomas in 1970 exported to the United States some 3,850,000 finished movements, put together with parts imported primarily from Japan, West Germany, and France. Tariff regulations make this worldwide shuttling profitable. If a licensed Virgin Islands manufacturer can turn out a product containing no more than 50 percent imported raw materials, he may ship it duty-free to the United States.

Because its industries are concentrated in a fractional part of the island's area, I feel that St. Croix is still much more attuned to its West Indian planter past than to modern America. Many ruins have been rebuilt into charming residences.

Typical is a great house restored by Lee Platt, an old sailing friend from New England who "swallowed the anchor" when he discovered St. Croix.

In 1965 Lee showed me pictures of the ruined mansion as it appeared when he first came upon it—a shell of stone fashioned by skilled slave masons, but little else. The roof had fallen in; floors and other woodwork had rotted away. Through Lee's loving care it has blossomed anew into a design for living, as it had once been for a long-departed planter family.

Curious, I asked Lee why he had chosen to make St. Croix his home. He made an eloquent gesture, encompassing his house and all the varied topography of the island plus the surrounding sea.

"Here is continuity," he replied, "a feeling of belonging some place that has stayed the same for a long time. St. Croix is a family island. Those of us who have settled here want to keep it that way."

St. Thomas offers a complete change of pace. So many cruise ships arrive that frequently the wharf cannot accommodate all of them, and late arrivals must lie anchored. Overhead, jets and lesser planes shuttle between the mainland and the surrounding islands. One-day tourists, stopover visitors, and residents alike flood from the narrow, crowded sidewalks into the streets,

memory work for the plant, but I have to do the thinking and set the controls."

Bauxite comes from Africa and Australia to Harvey's man-made harbor—once a mangrove swamp—and the alumina is shipped to the United States and Norway.

In a neighboring port created by Hess Oil Virgin Islands Corp., tankers from Venezuela, Africa, and the Middle East discharge crude oil. A refinery produces 205,000 barrels of petroleum products daily. The harbor is being dredged to take ships of 60-foot draught, so 250,000-ton supertankers will be able to call.

Hess Oil pays to the Virgin Islands government a daily royalty of $7,500 to be used for conservation and recreational facilities. It also conducts courses in mechanics, welding, and electronics. The new class had 107 students, all Virgin Islanders. On finishing, they are free to work for anyone they choose. Many of the earlier graduates have doubled their incomes.

There is also a thriving business in watch

where jammed-up taxis hoot them back.

The capital city Charlotte Amalie has shops stocked with almost every conceivable temptation. With its steel bands, nightclubs, French restaurants, and its bounty of bikinis, St. Thomas is the "swinger" of the three sister islands. This rollicking atmosphere is a heritage of the days when Denmark, as a neutral nation in the ever-recurring wars of Europe, threw its chief West Indian port open to all, including privateers and pirates. As my 1818 volume of *New Sailing Directions* put it, the city was a center of "such traffic as the French, English, Dutch, and Spaniards dare not carry on publicly in their own islands."

The city fathers of Charlotte Amalie in the early days asked no questions about the source of goods that filled the warehouses. "A privateer can use the harbor as long as he likes, but a pirate may not lie there more than 24 hours," wrote a planter, Johan Carstens, in the 1740's; he then defined the difference as he saw it: "A pirate is one who robs both ship and crew, and then kills the men; the privateer takes ship and cargo, and robs the men, but spares their lives."

Such distinctions rarely troubled the authorities. Some "Brethren of the Coast" even settled down to life ashore. Dominating Charlotte Amalie from a bluff is Bluebeard's Castle, where a pirate of that name supposedly maintained a lookout tower. It is now a hotel.

On a nearby eminence stood the stronghold of Edward Teach, better known as Blackbeard, one of the most thoroughgoing rascals in buccaneer history. One of his amusements was creating a miniature version of hell aboard his ship by battening the hatches and igniting sulphur below decks; he then led his crew down to see who could take it the longest. Until his head finally decorated the bowsprit of a Royal Navy sloop, there were those who believed Blackbeard the devil incarnate.

207

Wares from the world over stock the shopping streets of Charlotte Amalie, a free port on St. Thomas. Scandinavian imports fill shelves of the shop above. Islanders enjoy home-grown products—"drinking coconuts" and plantains ready for cooking.

St. Thomas has always been oriented more to the sea than to the land. The principal reason the United States acquired it and its sister islands during World War I was to secure the magnificent harbor of Charlotte Amalie as a naval base controlling the sea approaches to the Panama Canal. Thus, after purchase from Denmark on March 31, 1917, the Virgin Islands were governed by U. S. Navy officers until 1931, when President Herbert Hoover appointed a civilian governor.

As an unincorporated territory, the islands became wards of the Department of Interior. Residents were able to vote for a unicameral legislature, but not for the President of the United States or for Congressmen—or even their own Governor. But now this has changed. In 1970 islanders gained the right to elect their Governor and chose Melvin H. Evans, the United States' first elected black Governor. Other electoral reforms allowing a voice in national affairs are under consideration.

While islanders pay income taxes at the same rates as other U. S. citizens, the money is applied to local government projects.

However, residents and visitors alike enjoy a tariff break. Former Governor Ralph Paiewonsky explained: "St. Thomas was known as a free port under the Danes, with only a flat 6-percent levy on foreign goods. When the islands became American, Congress made U. S. goods duty-free, and kept the old 6-percent import tariff, which is far less on the average than mainland rates."

During the fiscal year ending June 30, 1969, St. Thomas was booming, even though it lacked major industry. Visitors numbered more than 1,122,000, an increase of nearly 200,000 over the previous year. Virgin Islands Department of Commerce figures showed a rise in tourist spending during the same period from $75,000,000 to $112,000,000.

The demand for workers was so great that outsiders outnumbered islanders in the labor force. Immigration laws had been relaxed to provide the services and skills vital to the boom. Often I felt that people born in the Virgin Islands were as rare as true New Yorkers in Manhattan. During my stay, hotel maids from Tortola cleaned my room when I spent a night ashore;

209

waiters from St. Kitts served my meals; taxi drivers were frequently from Anguilla or Montserrat. I met welders from Trinidad, mechanics from Barbados, and oil-refinery technicians from Aruba. So many Puerto Ricans have moved to St. Croix that Spanish is almost a second language.

Despite the bustle, Charlotte Amalie retains much flavor from its past. It rises on three hills, shown as Government, Berg, and French on modern maps, but called Mizzentop, Maintop, and Foretop in wind-

jammer days. Some streets, too steep for paving, remain flights of steps. Behind the waterfront, many warehouses have been converted into attractive stores and boutiques, with flowering alleyways between.

Since much of St. Thomas is as hilly as the capital, the island has been handicapped ever since its settlement by a lack of flat land for industry or agriculture; many early colonists moved on to the other islands to seek more easily tilled fields. Today the steep contours make it difficult to find areas

Lights of Charlotte Amalie star the darkening hills around Yacht Haven, where Sans Terre *moored off U. S.-owned St. Thomas at the end of the island cruise.*
JOHN LAUNOIS, BLACK STAR

for industry, and locating an airport capable of handling larger jets is the foremost headache of local planning groups.

The same rugged slopes are ideal for home-seekers. Houses perched like ospreys' nests command breath-stopping panoramas. From the highest peaks along our route, the British Virgins seemed like a handful of emeralds scattered on blue velvet by a careless pirate.

As sunset tinted the skies over Charlotte Amalie harbor, and myriad lights began to wink on the slopes, I remembered the words of Premier Eric Gairy in Grenada: "There have been more changes in the last four years than in the last century."

Or perhaps, I thought, than in the centuries going all the way back to the arrival of man after nature had finished her task of modeling a paradise on earth. Yet the paradise is still there, laved by limpid water, smiled upon by the sun, caressed by balmy breezes, the gently curving chain known as the Isles of the Caribbees.

Index

Illustrations references, including legends, appear in *italics*

Additional References

For related reading, you may wish to refer to the following NATIONAL GEOGRAPHIC articles:

Allmon, Gwen Drayton, "Martinique: A Tropical Bit of France," February 1959; Cerruti, James, "The Netherlands Antilles: Holland in the Caribbean," January 1970; Mitchell, Carleton, "*Carib* Cruises the West Indies," January 1948; "*Finisterre* Sails the Windward Islands," December 1965; "A Fresh Breeze Stirs the Leewards," October 1966; "Our Virgin Islands, 50 Years Under the Flag," January 1968; Scofield, John, "Virgin Islands: Tropical Playland, U. S. A.," February 1956.

For additional related material the following books are suggested:

Aspinall, Sir Algernon Edward, *The Pocket Guide to the West Indies and British Guiana, British Honduras, Bermuda, the Spanish Main, Surinam, the Panama Canal,* 10th edition, 1960; Burns, Sir Alan Cuthbert, *History of the British West Indies,* second edition, 1965; Creque, Darwin D., *The U. S. Virgins and the Eastern Caribbean,* 1968; Eggleston, George T., *Orchids on the Calabash Tree,* 1962; Fermor, Patrick Leigh, *The Traveller's Tree,* 1950; Harman, Jeanne Perkins, *The Virgins: Magic Islands,* 1961; Keur, John Y. and Dorothy, *Windward Children,* 1960; Macpherson, John, *Caribbean Lands: a geography of the West Indies,* 1965; Mitchell, Carleton, *Islands to Windward,* 1955; Rigg, J. Linton, *The Alluring Antilles,* 1963; Roberts, W. Adolphe, *The French in the West Indies,* 1942; Waugh, Alec, *A Family of Islands,* 1964.

Composition for Isles of the Caribbees by National Geographic's Phototypographic Division, John E. McConnell, Manager. Printed and bound by Fawcett Printing Corp., Rockville, Md. Color separations by The Lanman Co., Alexandria, Va.; Beck Engraving Co., Philadelphia, Pa.; and Graphic Color Plate, Inc., Stamford, Conn.